4/15/14

James,

To a legendary

and inspiring leader...

wishing you great

success with your

next chapter!

All my best

Additional praise for *Confessions of a Successful CIO: How the Best CIOs Tackle Their Toughest Business Challenges*

"Everyone knows we learn best by experience. But not everyone has the opportunity to have so many experiences. The best of us learn from other people's experiences, in addition to our own. This collection of stories of leadership moments faced by giants in our field is a great opportunity to grow."

> **— June Drewry, Director of the Society for Information Management's Leadership Development Institute and former Global CIO, Chubb, Aon, and Lincoln National**

"I enjoyed reading the CIO confessions; real, insightful, and inspiring stories of leadership, across the challenging and broad spectrum of business, people, process, and technology aspects of today's CIO responsibilities in forward-thinking corporations. Each story provides relevant approaches and examples of personal behavior for successful, and in some cases bold, leadership at the complex intersection of technology and business. The practical and no-nonsense story-telling triggers reflection and comparisons with similar situations any CIO will encounter and is helpful to formulate the right style and approach, or validate the chosen path to sustainable business value creation and personal success."

> **— Roland Paanakker, former CIO, Nike Inc.**

"In *Confessions of a Successful CIO*, the authors present tremendous insights into the philosophy and approaches of a set of truly world-class CIOs. Their stories are incredibly insightful, following their journeys through challenging, big-bet situations that they converted into major opportunities to support the transformation of their organizations. The stories so poignantly illustrate the critical leadership approaches that these CIOs employed to achieve amazing results. These stories provide any current or aspiring CIO with incredible examples of how to truly achieve the full potential of IT in their organizations."

> **—Steve Morin, CIO, Bright Horizon**

"*Confessions of a Successful CIO* is a compilation of genuine and inspirational stories sure to motivate IT leaders in pursuit of achieving transformational successes. The influential CIOs profiled in this book tell their stories with such authenticity; you will feel invigorated and challenged to pursue excellence in your own career."

> **—Mary Gendron, Senior Vice President and CIO, Celestica**

"*Confessions of a Successful CIO* is filled with a ton of insightful leadership lessons and real, actionable advice necessary for the modern-day CIO to be successful, as told through the stories of top-flight CIO leaders. A must-read for those already in the role—and certainly for those who aspire to be IT leaders."

> **—Stuart Kippelman, CIO, Covanta Energy**

"Each story provides 'real world' experiences, along with leadership wisdom and a boost of energy, for what all IT organizations are trying to do today–create value. This is a great reminder that the role of CIO is not for the faint of heart, but with courage and leadership great things can and do happen."

> **—Dede Ramoneda, Group Vice President and CIO, First Citizens Bank**

"The job of a CIO is becoming increasingly demanding and challenging, no matter what vertical industry you may be a part of. In this book, we have the opportunity to read the stories told by some of the most exemplary CIOs out there, who not only faced up to the demands and challenges but created excitingly innovative approaches to high-stakes situations that would likely make or break their careers. If you are a CIO, this book will both inspire you and challenge you to new ways of thinking."

—David L. Miller, Vice Chancellor and CIO,
University of Arkansas for Medical Sciences

"*Confessions of Successful CIO* shares mini-epic stories to visualize real time, tough business problems and how persevering high-powered CIOs solve issues to reach business goals. As an IT executive, placing the art of IT over the science of IT demystifies how we all can reach the best outcomes with our customers and business value."

—Ben Berry, Chief Technology Officer, City of Portland

"Roberts and Watson have done a terrific job capturing these virtues with inspirational lessons from some of the top CIOs in the business. Taking advantage of the knowledge and wisdom collected within is like a baseball player getting batting tips from 10 of the best hitters in the game!"

— Jay Ferro, CIO, American Cancer Society

"The testimonials are great, packed with insights that are highly transferable across industries. The method of transferring these insights through the stories of life experiences makes them memorable and actionable with immediate applicability and impact."

—James Swanson, CIO, Monsanto

"The natural, story-type flow about these CIOs is easy to consume, and readers can really relate to their stories and principles. At times it seemed like a mirror to some of my own experiences and very good net/simplification of the principles of a CIO role in today's world: people and leadership first, truly engaging in the business, and driving transformational changes to the portfolio that clearly impact revenue, costs, and client retention."

—Mike Gioja, CIO/Senior Vice President IT,
Product Management & Development, Paychex

"When it comes to pragmatic advice, this book is it! *Confessions of a Successful CIO* focuses on translating the experiences of successful CIOs into attributes of success. A more traditional CIO can get caught up in the focus of the Big Four: Social, Mobile, Cloud, and Big Data. This book, however, appropriately places the focus on the leadership required and the roles needed to organize and utilize technology for competitive advantage. It takes bold leadership to recognize the power of technology to enable business results. The collection of experiences presented in this book provides insight for CIOs and other executives to adopt in their personal quest to bring transformative change to the customer experience, operational capability, and shareholder results. Readers will find the necessary tools to navigate the C-suite, the courage to make a difference, and the inspiration to focus on what matters most."

—Victor Fetter, CIO and Managing Director, LPL Financial

"The lessons detailed by the various CIOs caused me to think of several similar and daunting challenges in my own career as a CIO. Once again, the lessons learned are valuable and they should be repeated: work closely with your clients, focus on the bottom-line of the organization, and always move toward 'how am I going to contribute to team success?'. This book inspires me to reenergize myself and the team through exemplary leadership and contribution to organizational success. If I don't contribute significantly as a leader, someone else surely will (and, that's bad)."

—Scott Culbertson, Vice President/CIO, UGI Utilities

CONFESSIONS OF A
SUCCESSFUL CIO

Founded in 1807, John Wiley & Sons is the oldest independent publishing company in the United States. With offices in North America, Europe, Asia, and Australia, Wiley is globally committed to developing and marketing print and electronic products and services for our customers' professional and personal knowledge and understanding.

The Wiley CIO series provides information, tools, and insights to IT executives and managers. The products in this series cover a wide range of topics that supply strategic and implementation guidance on the latest technology trends, leadership, and emerging best practices.

Titles in the Wiley CIO series include:

The Agile Architecture Revolution: How Cloud Computing, REST-Based SOA, and Mobile Computing Are Changing Enterprise IT by Jason Bloomberg

Architecting the Cloud: Design Decisions for Cloud Computing Service Models (SaaS, PaaS, and IaaS) by Michael Kavis

Big Data, Big Analytics: Emerging Business Intelligence and Analytic Trends for Today's Businesses by Michael Minelli, Michele Chambers, and Ambiga Dhiraj

The Chief Information Officer's Body of Knowledge: People, Process, and Technology by Dean Lane

CIO Best Practices: Enabling Strategic Value with Information Technology (Second Edition) by Joe Stenzel, Randy Betancourt, Gary Cokins, Alyssa Farrell, Bill Flemming, Michael H. Hugos, Jonathan Hujsak, and Karl Schubert

The CIO Playbook: Strategies and Best Practices for IT Leaders to Deliver Value by Nicholas R. Colisto

Decoding the IT Value Problem: An Executive Guide for Achieving Optimal ROI on Critical IT Investments by Gregory J. Fell

Enterprise Performance Management Done Right: An Operating System for Your Organization by Ron Dimon

Information Governance: Concepts, Strategies and Best Practices by Robert F. Smallwood

CONFESSIONS OF A SUCCESSFUL CIO

HOW THE BEST CIOs TACKLE THEIR TOUGHEST BUSINESS CHALLENGES

Dan Roberts

Brian P. Watson

WILEY

Published by John Wiley & Sons, Inc., Hoboken, New Jersey.
Published simultaneously in Canada.

For general information on our other products and services or for technical support, please
contact our Customer Care Department within the United States at (800) 762-2974, outside
the United States at (317) 572-3993 or fax (317) 572-4002.

Wiley publishes in a variety of print and electronic formats and by print-on-demand. Some
material included with standard print versions of this book may not be included in e-books or in
print-on-demand. If this book refers to media such as a CD or DVD that is not included in the
version you purchased, you may download this material at http://booksupport.wiley.com. For
more information about Wiley products, visit www.wiley.com.

Library of Congress Cataloging-in-Publication Data:

Roberts, Dan (Dan D.), 1963–
    Confessions of a successful CIO : how the best CIOs tackle their toughest business
challenges / Dan Roberts, Brian P. Watson.
       pages   cm. — (The Wiley CIO series)
    Includes bibliographical references and index.
    ISBN 978-1-118-63822-4 (hardback) — ISBN 978-1-118-84930-9 (ePDF) —
    ISBN 978-1-118-84928-6 (ePub)
       1. Chief information officers.   2. Information technology—Management.
3. Chief information officers—Case studies.   4. Information technology—Management—
Case studies.   I. Watson, Brian P., 1978   II. Title.
HD30.2.R6275 2014
658.4'038—dc23

                                                              2014000598

Printed in the United States of America
10 9 8 7 6 5 4 3 2 1

To the men and women of our armed forces, active or veteran. And to organizations such as Workforce Opportunity Services (WOS) and Darkhorse Benefits, who are committed to helping our veterans build strong corporate careers, leveraging their unique values and competencies in the private sector—and, once again, building an even stronger America.

CONTENTS

FOREWORD

I love this book. It's informative, inspirational, and memorable. Each chapter reads like a mini suspense novel, complete with heroes, villains, and cliffhangers. It's not really a book, but a compilation of stories about leaders who have transformed their companies with technology. As a reader, I felt like I was in the inside circle, privy to information usually shared over a drink.

The leaders profiled within did more than they thought they could in situations that are more challenging than most. We learn from their mistakes and successes, and are emboldened by their courage and discipline. The narrative format allows us to record the stories neatly away in our memories, allowing us to hit "replay" when we need them the most.

Leading with technology is, first and foremost, about leadership. While there is no one-size-fits-all road to success, great leaders, like the ones profiled within this book, are marked by a unique set of qualities: passion and drive to make a positive difference, the ability to engage others to chart the future and define the path, and the paradoxical ability to maintain optimism and perseverance through difficult circumstances.

With courageous and disciplined leadership as the foundation, the other factor that distinguishes these leaders is a level of technology smarts that is only born from experience. Technology-smart leaders know how to identify (in the words of one of the CIOs profiled here) the "art of the possible" amid the complex assortment of desired outcomes, existing capabilities and complexities, and various resources—technical and organizational—that can be applied to the transformational journey.

As described within, the art of the possible entails placing big bets and buying down risks by emphasizing people over process. This is an important message, one that is largely missing from the left-brain-oriented literature that dominates the technology press. Do a tag cloud on this book, and words like *business*, *team*, and *people* will dominate, while *service catalog, architecture*, and *process* appear in the background, if at all.

These pages include timeless lessons on how to exploit technology to the benefit of the business and the people within. This isn't simply a book for CIOs or technology professionals. For large businesses or small—or somewhere in between—managing technology assets is an essential part of everyone's job, and absorbing the insights of this book will give leaders a realistic picture of what it takes to exploit technology and transform businesses.

Get ready to hunker down and learn from the best. Keep your pen close at hand, as you will want to underline and notate insights that resonate and ideas that ignite. Put yourself in the shoes of the leader. Pause at the key decision points and decide for yourself what goals you would set and how you would proceed before turning the pages and letting the story unfold.

These novelettes will encourage you to strive to be best version of yourself. They will inform, challenge, and inspire you to work even harder to become the leader you were uniquely created to be.

Use what you learn to enrich your own leadership narrative. Brian, Dan, and I look forward to reading about it!

Susan Cramm
Leadership Coach and Author,
8 Things We Hate About I.T.:
How to Move Beyond the Frustrations
and Form a New Partnership with I.T.

PREFACE

Welcome to *Confessions of a Successful CIO*. Early warning: This isn't your normal book on IT leadership.

Most books in this category focus on a theory—very smart people espousing their ideas about the CIO role, how it will change, what current and aspiring IT leaders must do to succeed. Those books are valuable, and they provide an inordinate amount of useful, actionable ideas for today's IT leaders.

We might have our own ideas about those things, but we thought it best to leave the theory to smarter folks. We came up with a different approach: Find the best CIOs in the United States—arguably, in the world—and tell their stories.

What do we mean by "stories?" It's relatively simple: We asked these respected, acclaimed IT leaders to walk us through the toughest business challenge they've ever faced, how they tackled it, and what they learned from it. The stories we heard—and that you're about to read—are, simply put, awe-inspiring. We've been working with or writing about IT leadership for more than 35 years combined, but the stories in this book were beyond what we expected—and will continue to amaze for a very long time.

All that said, the hardest task was selecting those CIOs. We may have years of experience interfacing with them, but we knew we couldn't take on such a task alone. There's another piece of magic in this book: To pick these CIOs, we called on some of the most prominent thought leaders in the CIO universe to help us pick our nine.

Meet our expert panel:

- Susan Cramm, who graciously wrote the Foreword, is the author of the acclaimed book, *8 Things We Hate About I.T.* A former CFO and CIO, Susan provides executive coaching to Fortune 500 companies and writes a blog for *Strategy+Business*.
- Shawn Banerji is a managing director in the Global Technology Sector at Russell Reynolds Associates. He is a

senior member of the firm's Information Officers Practice and a trusted advisor to global corporations seeking the IT leadership to transform and optimize their businesses. Shawn is frequently sought out by both the media and academia as a thought leader on the CIO role.

- Gary Beach is publisher emeritus of *CIO Magazine* and has spent more than 30 years analyzing the CIO role. His book, *The U.S. Technology Skills Gap*, was a business best seller in 2013.

- Barbra Cooper spent more than 30 years in IT leadership in the financial, technology, government, and automotive sectors. She retired in 2013 after serving as CIO of Toyota Motor Sales and was inducted into the CIO Hall of Fame in 2007.

- Peter High is president of Metis Strategy, an IT strategy consultancy that counts some of the world's elite IT leaders as clients. He analyzes the CIO role for the Forbes CIO Network and hosts the Forum on World Class IT podcast, an offshoot of his best-selling book, *World Class IT: How Business Succeeds When Technology Triumphs*.

- Art Langer is academic director and faculty member of the Master of Science in Technology Management Program at Columbia University and a contributor to the *Wall Street Journal's CIO Journal*. Art is also founder and chairman of Workforce Opportunity Services, a 501(c)(3) nonprofit.

In working with these all-stars—and hearing their no-holds-barred input—we decided on a few things in terms of criteria. We could just go to the top Fortune 500 companies and interview their CIOs, but we decided, in this case, that size doesn't matter. Sure, some of the CIOs in this book come from large companies, household names, or recognizable brands, but that's not what got them here.

What got them here is simple. They're leaders, not techies. They talk business, not bits and bytes. The CIO of today—and most certainly of the future—needs to navigate the C-suite the same way the other occupants do. Pride in the function is commendable, but not if it stops there.

Once we chose the CIOs, we interviewed them to get the inside story of their own biggest business challenges. The stories we heard were incredible, and in them, we heard several major themes repeatedly:

- **Bet the farm.** These leaders are not afraid to take on the big risks. They're not afraid to pitch the big ideas, because they know they can speak the language and justify the investment.
- **Answer the call.** These leaders stepped up when they were called to action—oftentimes to help save their companies' futures. This requires a confidence in their abilities, and in their own experiences, that not every leader has.
- **People come first.** These leaders understand the value their people bring to their organization. They don't treat them like a number or an interchangeable part.
- **Decisiveness makes all the difference.** Despite their human side, these leaders understand that they need to make tough decisions that affect not only their people but also their company's health.
- **Results matter.** These leaders don't do pie-in-the-sky research and development or implement the latest bright, shiny objects without knowing the business case and the long-term business value. They're more focused on enabling and improving the business and on driving the all-important metrics that do that.

So, in the end, maybe there is a theory. The best IT leaders do all those things.

And by telling their stories, we hope that the current and future generations of IT leaders will use these case studies to learn, to teach, to inspire, and to elevate our profession to higher, more game-changing levels.

ACKNOWLEDGMENTS

Dan and Brian would like to thank: The 9 "Bet-the-Farm" CIOs who make this book what it is. Although exceptionally busy, each made the time to participate in the spirit of paying it forward to the next generation of leaders. All of these phenomenal leaders brings their own vision, perspective, and leadership style to everything they do, but as a unit, they are the oracles and instructors for any and all who hope to rise to the CIO level. One of their most striking attributes is their ability to answer the call when their businesses need them most. We're just happy they answered ours and so humbly shared their stories, successes, and failures.

Our expert panel, who collectively and individually helped us identify the CIOs in this book, giving us the perspective we needed going in and the validation we needed along the way. Shawn Banerji, Gary Beach, Barbra Cooper, Peter High, and Art Langer are fantastic thought leaders and representatives of this noble community we call home, and we have the greatest appreciation for their contributions.

Susan Cramm, another member of our expert panel, graciously wrote our Foreword. She's one of the smartest, sharpest people in the executive leadership arena, and we're thankful for all the great contributions Susan has made to current and future IT leaders. And we're incredibly thankful that she made the time to be a constant source of enthusiasm and encouragement throughout the writing process (and way, way before). And she happens to be the genius who came up with the title!

To folks like June Drewry, Abbie Lundberg, David Buckholtz, Steve Morin, Susan Courtney, Dennis L'Heureux, Mary Gendron, Jay Ferro, David Miller, Stu Kippelman, Mike Gioja, James Swanson, Ben Berry, and Susan Nakashima, who offered steady support for our efforts and were kind enough to provide inspiring reviews. You really gave us a great energy boost as we pushed toward the end zone.

■ ■ ■

Dan would like to thank: My phenomenal team at Ouellette & Associates—I have worked with many of you for more years than any of us will admit. I so appreciate your dedication to your craft and commitment to improving our profession. A big thank-you goes to Tracy Dinu and Karen Keller, who supported this book project in so many ways, from brainstorming around the conference room table to finished product.

My very talented coauthor Brian Watson—what a great ride and collaboration. As this project came together in my head, I knew this book was yours to write. Your ability to capture the story-within-the-story and the personalities of those you interview is a gift that I marvel at. So, what's next?

My "Special Ks," Kristina and Kelly—you have made me the proudest dad! You have grown into amazing, motivated people whom I admire and respect. You are going to do great things in this world, and you have no idea how much you inspire me every day.

My incredible wife of 28 years, Denise—you encourage me, support me, push me, and yes, tolerate me and my crazy schedule and travel that allows me to do the work I so enjoy. Without you, I am nothing, and I love and appreciate you more than you will ever know.

■ ■ ■

Brian would like to thank: All of my colleagues at Workforce Opportunity Services and each one of the military veterans and budding corporate all-stars who have been through our programs—you all inspire me in ways that you can't even imagine.

Special thanks to my good buddy Pete Van Emburgh, who was gracious enough to dust off his journalist cap to help me find my voice in the initial chapters—just like he did during our long hours in the Roberts Hall basement editing *The Bucknellian*.

My former editor and one of my journalistic idols, Tom Steinert-Threlkeld, who left this world way too early in October 2013. Tom—or TST, as we all knew him—gave me the opportunity to write columns about this book and some of the great people in it for CruxialCIO.com. He is and will be missed by so many.

My coauthor Dan Roberts, who, despite being in a different locale, was in the foxhole with me, envisioning each chapter from start to finish and adding his own unique "special sauce" to what you're about to read.

The people who taught me how to write: my mom, Kathy Watson; my dad, Charlie Watson; and my brother, Chuck Watson; Bro. George Zehnle, S.M.; John Rickard; John McCormick; and Stephan Garnett. Hopefully, the imperfections in this book aren't an insult to the amazing presence you've played in my life, my growth, and how I write about this wild world we live in.

And my wife, Carrie, for putting up with my long hours at the dining room table, grinding away at each chapter. For the never-ending stories I told you about all of them. For letting me ramble on about each one. Your smiles, encouragement, and love made this book happen—and I'll never stop reminding you of that.

CHAPTER 1

The Anticipator: Filippo Passerini

The weather in Athens, Greece, is pretty nice late in the year. At the very least, it's a whole lot nicer there than in Cincinnati, Ohio.

It was a Friday evening in September 2002. Filippo Passerini—then serving as the Athens-based vice president of marketing operations and corporate marketing team leader for Western Europe for Procter & Gamble (P&G)—got a call from corporate headquarters in Cincinnati. It was the morning, Eastern Standard Time.

P&G's second in command asked him about his wife and family, and how he was enjoying his assignment in Greece. Passerini thanked him and exchanged pleasantries, but after 20 minutes of idle chitchat, he knew something was up.

"What do you really want?" Passerini asked the executive.

The answer to this question was more complex. At the time, P&G was in the midst of an extremely complicated situation regarding their shared services organization. The company had decided to investigate opportunities to monetize the unit. But the deal was becoming too complex, and employees were frightened about their futures.

Would Passerini have any problem curtailing his assignment in Greece sooner than expected to help fix the problem? How soon? "Monday."

Passerini was in a line-management role, another step in a deep rotation through P&G's business—the kind of opportunity that, given two seconds to think about it, any aspiring C-level executive would drool over. He had a made a clear decision to see his assignment through—and to stay away from his background in IT for a few years to get a broader view of business leadership.

The shared services project needed leadership, and Passerini knew it. He was far across the Atlantic, but word spread. Many of the 7,500 people in the organization were voicing heavyhearted concerns about their future.

And Passerini and his family were reveling in their life in Athens. Yet there he was, on a plane back to Cincinnati that weekend, about to embark on a journey that would lead him to perhaps the most prestigious role of any information technology leader in the world.

■ ■ ■

Passerini, a native of Rome, Italy, began his corporate career with Procter & Gamble in November 1981. The 24-year-old systems analyst climbed the corporate ladder quickly, rising through the IT organization until being named vice president in 1997.

He served in leadership capacities—in IT and various line-management functions—on four continents before taking the helm of P&G's Global Business Services (GBS) division in 2003 and being appointed chief information officer the following year. Today he sits as group president, Global Business Services, and CIO of the $83 billion maker of some of the world's most recognizable consumer brands.

His long-term performance—particularly, his prowess for innovating and creating real business value—have garnered him more awards than he can probably count, including *InformationWeek*'s 2010 "Chief of the Year" and the inaugural Fisher-Hopper Prize for Lifetime Achievement in CIO Leadership from the University of California–Berkeley's Haas School of Business.

But his ascendancy to that role began with that fateful phone call from Cincinnati in 2002.

A few years earlier, Passerini was watching the IT industry turn on its head. The dot-com boom suddenly went bust. Start-ups, promising new technologies and capabilities to power the era of e-commerce, gobbled up millions upon millions in venture capital money, only to disappear seemingly a month later. Jobs disappeared just as quickly, setting the United States off toward its most turbulent economic decade in more than 50 years.

But there was a silver lining for some: Spending on IT infrastructure and services was projected to rise at a steady clip.

A. G. Lafley, P&G's acclaimed two-time chairman and CEO, and Roger Martin, Dean of the Rotman School of Management at the University of Toronto (and longtime adviser to Lafley), document this period succinctly in their recent book, *Playing to Win: How Strategy Really Works* (Harvard Business Press, 2013). As those demands grew, in came a new crop of providers—both domestic and foreign—called business process outsourcers (BPOs). "As the post-crash dust cleared, rapidly digitizing companies were faced with decisions on how much to use BPOs, which BPO partner to select, and how best to do so," Lafley and Martin explained. "It wasn't easy; the implications of a poor choice could be millions of dollars in extra costs and untold headaches down the line."

In 1999, P&G created its GBS organization, essentially pulling together under one umbrella the units it thought could be outsourced. These included IT, facilities management, and employee services. Three years later, the company evaluated three options for the department's future: keep it in-house, spin it off into a separate BPO, or outsource most of it to one of the active players in the BPO arena.

There was no clear or easy decision. Many at P&G saw an arduous path ahead. Passerini saw an opportunity.

■ ■ ■

One of the most important motivators for Passerini in this project was the notion of turning a problem into an opportunity. It was something he experienced—the hard way—10 years into what is now his 31-year tenure at P&G.

From his start in Italy, Passerini went to Turkey as a manager of management systems. He moved from there, in 1991, to the United Kingdom, where P&G had its second-largest IT operation, as well as its second-largest profit center. In the United Kingdom, Passerini had to step up what he called his broken English to the Queen's English. At the same time, most of the team members he was overseeing there were older than he was.

Then P&G decided it would roll out a new order-to-cash system across Europe. The system was the backbone—the veritable nerve center—of everything P&G does, from orders to pricing to payment to the biggest of all: shipping. If P&G can't ship its products, P&G products don't land on store shelves. If P&G products aren't on the store shelves, P&G isn't selling.

Passerini volunteered to handle the first rollout. "I thought I could easily conquer the world," he said. But this was no conquest. The rollout went very badly, Passerini said, mainly due to his inability to adequately manage both the change and the expectations. He thought he was finished at P&G. He even went home and told his wife they'd probably need to head back to Italy to find another job.

Clearly, it wasn't so. Passerini turned it around, and two years later, he was promoted to director and sent to Latin America. He turned a bad situation into a positive one, and now he drills that ethic into the heads of everyone in his GBS organization. "It's more than fixing the issue. It's not about playing an even game. If you are 1–0, to use soccer language, it's not only about how to get to 1–1, but how can you win the game?" Passerini said. "When we have an issue, we always think not just how to fix it, but how to turn a negative perception of a system problem or change management into a success story. This is another element, from a cultural standpoint, that is so critical."

Fast-forward to Cincinnati, where Passerini was beginning to assess what to do with GBS. The three options were on the table: stay the course, spin it out, or outsource it. According to Lafley and Martin, "Any of these choices might have seemed sensible given the circumstances. But none effectively answered the question of how P&G could win with its global services."

The leadership team overseeing the outsourcing idea decided, after a long selection process and negotiations, to sell the unit to Electronic Data Systems, then a leader in the BPO space. But that created negative reactions among GBS employees, whose futures became uncertain and confused. In turn, that started a lot of internal swirl.

GBS employees were in disarray. Would they have jobs? If they stayed with P&G, what roles would they be given? Company leaders were getting hundreds of messages a day from these frightened employees.

Things were spinning out of control. Passerini knew he needed to find a different solution, an alternative to the three options put on the table. And the GBS employees would need a little tough love.

■ ■ ■

Ask anyone who knows Filippo Passerini, and they'll tell you he's one of the nicest guys you'll meet in the business. But he's also a firm believer in tough love.

That term means a lot of things to a lot of people, and most of the time it's just some jargon from business school that seems to fit the occasion. But for Passerini, it's a mind-set, a modus operandi for dealing with 6,000-odd people he oversees globally today at P&G.

As he continued to review the options, he saw pluses and minuses, as Lafley and Martin described.

Since the entire issue created so much dissension, they could always keep GBS internally. This was the "if it ain't broke, don't fix it" option. Selling the unit to a BPO would make a big splash, but it could have the negative effect on morale that Passerini was hearing. Outsourcing to EDS or another major BPO offered economies of scale, but would P&G see the cost-effectiveness and service levels it required? Would outsourcing really create an environment that fostered innovation and value creation?

When there's no easy answer, leaders have to get creative. Passerini came up with a better option: "selective" outsourcing. Instead of going with one BPO, he decided to selectively partner each area with best-in-class providers.

"The logic of this best-of-breed option was that P&G's needs are highly varied and that a variety of more specialized partners would be most capable of meeting the needs," Lafley and Martin wrote. "Passerini saw that specialization could increase the quality and lower the cost of BPO solutions, and believed that P&G could manage the complexity of multiple relationships to create more value than it could through one relationship." The selective option also limited risk across partners and gave P&G a clearer baseline for their performance.

GBS outsourced IT support and applications to Hewlett-Packard (HP), then only fourth in the market. Employee services went to IBM Global Services, and facilities management to Jones Lang LaSalle. The benefits to the company were beyond considerable: To date, P&G claims Passerini's GBS organization has saved the company more than $1 billion since this critical decision.

But as he knew, any decision at that point would yield some emotional responses from employees, given the deep concerns that many people had developed. When some asked why—after so many years of success—was P&G outsourcing at all, Passerini stood firm. He's not in the outsourcing-just-to-outsource camp; cost savings are important, but there were added benefits—benefits that would drive even more value for the company.

"It allowed us to completely reframe the way we think about our role within the business," Passerini said, 10 years after executing the selective outsourcing deal. "We have farmed out what we consider more of the mundane, commodity cost, and kept in-house the more upstream, strategic value-creation part of technology. And we did it because it would give us more flexibility, it is more strategic for P&G, and it allows us to focus on bigger ideas."

But the people issues remained. Passerini again stood firm.

Early into the process, he committed to working as quickly as possible to find the right solution and model to solve the GBS crisis. In the meantime, he knew that many P&G employees would be forced to move to other companies, so he worked to negotiate the best terms with the new service provider.

When HP won the IT business, 2,000 P&G employees made the transition—but with equal salary and benefits to those they had at P&G. So despite the turmoil and uncertainty, Passerini said, those employees landed parallel jobs at a top technology provider, and one that could probably offer very strong career opportunities.

"Tough love is important. I learned it's so crucial to give people full transparency about what is happening," Passerini said. "There is always a dilemma about how much you tell employees when you have a new idea, early on, because it may generate more questions and concerns than benefits. We have come to the conclusion that we share everything immediately . . . things may not always materialize, but we want our people to know that if it doesn't work, we will change again and do something different."

■ ■ ■

Passerini will be the first to tell you that he was not exactly welcomed by all when he took over leadership of GBS. Some people were happy, but others saw the appointment of Passerini—who came from outside GBS—as sending a negative message to the leadership of the GBS organization.

There are many ways to right that ship. But another decision Passerini made surprised many of his naysayers—and stood the chance of destroying any credibility he had.

After the decision was made to kill the deal with EDS, a governance committee P&G established to steer the project was dismantled. In the eyes of many within GBS, it was a victory, because this committee was seen as having taken over GBS during the deal. To Passerini, it was another opportunity.

The 15 members of the committee had been through quite a wringer prior to Passerini's arrival. They had deep experience and understanding of GBS. They were originally chosen because of their competence.

So he decided to invite them back into GBS. Passerini told his troops, quite simply, that it would be a waste to lose the group's knowledge. Not all of the 15 decided to come into GBS full-time, but Passerini was able to persuade the folks who fit best to join his organization.

That decision was critical to what happened next: executing the $4 billion selective outsourcing deal in only 11 months. The shadow committee had worked for 18 months on a solution, and they had crafted the proposal with EDS—the proposal that served as the blueprint for the IT outsourcing to HP.

■ ■ ■

Not long after the deal was done, GBS employees posed an interesting question to Passerini: "Are we done yet?" Passerini's answer goes to one of his fundamental leadership principles: staying relevant.

Passerini—adapting guidelines Lafley established for P&G executives in his "playing to win" philosophy—asks three major questions of his team before undertaking a major initiative.

The first is, what right does the organization have to win? When it comes to technology, too many CIOs think that buying the latest software or systems will automatically translate to business value. "CIOs will normally think, if I do what is right, it will translate to good for the business. We don't think so," he said. "We think you need to start with the end in mind of what is the business value, and then work backwards into all the steps that unequivocally lead to that business value creation."

But to get to that value creation, Passerini asks tough questions. Does his organization have better skills? Does his team have more passion?

The second is, what needs to happen for the initiative to generate that business value? "What needs to be drilled in to be successful?" Passerini asked. He forces his team to look beyond vendor buzz and spin—and also to acknowledge how fast business and technology are changing today.

The third is the most important: What can go wrong? Passerini says he lives his life by that critical question. And it helps his team understand the concept of *anticipating* issues before they spring up.

With those three—he calls them the rocks of his organization—he forces a larger discussion around relevance. "The only thing we're interested in is being relevant to the business—creating value for the business," Passerini said. "What can we do to be more relevant? This is a most critical question, and one that we should ask ourselves every day. "

So, when asked if the organization is done yet, Passerini points to relevance. Instead of thinking about the huge outsourcing deal that was just completed, he refocused his people on what was yet to come. They still had jobs to do, services to provide. If they could stay relevant, Passerini said, then the organization will prosper. "Our future, our destiny, is in our hands," he told his team.

But these weren't just casual (or popular) words of encouragement. He broke it down further—if GBS gets complacent or becomes a commodity, then they must compete with other providers in developing nations, and in the process, they'll lose confidence from the business. That's the opposite of the relevance he seeks.

"So the question for us is not whether or not there will be more outsourcing," Passerini said. "The question for us is, what needs to be true for us to stay relevant in the business? Otherwise we're at the mercy of 'anything can happen.'"

■ ■ ■

To Passerini, relevance needs to come with a certain degree of humility. He emphasizes to his team to not act like know-it-alls, but to also have the confidence to accept more responsibility and the self-assurance to propose innovative ideas to the business.

Relevance matters. If P&G's IT or GBS organizations weren't coming up with compelling and creative ideas that actually drive business results, then they surely would have been getting plenty of input from business leadership.

The relationship with senior leadership is built on trust—and credibility. One would have to think that's the case because of the success of the GBS organization since Passerini took the helm in 2003.

There were plenty of positive outcomes from the massive outsourcing deals P&G cut, but for Passerini, perhaps the biggest was the capacity to focus on doing what he preaches the most: adding value to the business. That came with farming out the "mundane" IT tasks so they could focus on more strategic undertakings. "It [gives] us more flexibility, it is more strategic for P&G, it allows us to focus on bigger ideas," he said.

Passerini and his team have built up a treasure trove of noteworthy innovations, but he doesn't dwell on any single technology-specific victory. Instead, he harkens back to the vision of making P&G the most digitally (read: technologically) powered corporation in the world.

One of the toughest things for any IT organization is to bring their accomplishments to life. Virtualization can increase server capacity, but that's not something users can touch and feel. Providing mobile access to corporate systems via smartphones and tablets is clearly tangible, but it's increasingly becoming table stakes for modern IT shops.

But walk around P&G's headquarters, and you will undoubtedly see technological innovation in ways that most never imagined 20 or even 10 years ago.

There's the Business Sphere, an oval conference room with wall-to-wall screens. When business teams take their seats, the screens light up, depicting a globe. An analyst takes them through how P&G products are selling in any location—from Pampers in Portugal to Downy in Denver. Executives can see just about real-time details on every facet of sales and make crucial decisions on supply chain, merchandising, and pricing. P&G has since deployed more than 50 Business Spheres around the world.

Then there are Decision Cockpits, which are something like dashboards on steroids they began developing in 2008. These portals—displaying the quasi-proverbial "single version of the truth"—harness data on business operations and trends, including automatic alerts and drilled-down analysis. End users can customize their portals to help them arrive at faster decisions. Initially, 2,000 used them on a weekly basis. To date, the cockpits have been rolled out to more than 58,000 team members.

Yet another example is virtual mock-ups, which presented a new way to think and rethink the way P&G packages and presents its brands on shelves. In the past, when the marketing team at a product like Tide wanted to redesign the packaging, they had no choice but to create a physical prototype. Then they had to get all the physical competitive products to see how the new design looked when stacked on shelves. Today, the designs are done virtually, allowing brand managers and their teams to make decisions without the cost and effort of creating an actual product. The old way could take more than a month; the new way happens in about two days.

■ ■ ■

Whatever the project or initiative, Passerini and his team play to win. They strive to innovate. And they don't stop until they've delivered real business value for P&G. The idea of anticipating is equally vital.

Passerini's emphasis on anticipation, in many ways, comes from an examination of history.

Think back to Detroit. Decades ago, a prevailing concept in business was the big fish devouring the small fish. You could see it with the then–Big Three car manufacturers. Their operations were integrated, more monolithic. They owned everything from the plants to the dealerships.

They had a staggering number of employees. Big fish, indeed, and they gobbled up all the upstart competitors who tried to stake a claim.

Then came the Japanese manufacturers, with a new model that stressed agility and flexibility in pricing, manufacturing, and marketing. Slowly but surely, the Big Three found their match. The big fish were strong, but the fast fish were taking over.

Today, Passerini sees a different playing field. To him, it's not about the big versus the small, or the fast versus the slow, but the ones that can network with others, instead of being trapped in the old ways.

The visual is a little harder to imagine, but anyone with even a cursory understanding of today's business environment can glom on pretty quickly. Most business executives neglect to take such an anecdotal view, but for Passerini, it's a reality he can't ignore—and he applies it to every aspect of his organization.

Plenty of CIOs staff up in the usual, classic IT skills like architecture, development, or project management. Passerini and his team continue to seek out IT professionals who can navigate this new, hyper-networked world. That means working with partners, managing relationships to a higher level of win-win outcomes. And he said his team finds this more exciting—which leads to higher morale.

This is where anticipation comes in: He saw the future before it arrived, thanks to the lessons of the past. And you know what they say about those who don't know history. . . .

"I've come to the conclusion that anticipating in life is fundamental to stay in control. This applies across most areas. Think about sports. Skiing, for example. If you're falling behind, you fall. If you're playing tennis, if you anticipate the ball just a bit, you have much more power," Passerini said. "It's about anticipating what's coming. If we anticipate, we stay in control."

It all circles back to getting ahead of the business, analyzing the overarching global trends that affect P&G's business, and creating solutions that keep the company ahead of its competitors. That ability to anticipate influenced his and P&G's belief in leading any initiative with the outcome they desire. When they know what they're after, they thrive—they play to win, as Lafley and Martin say—and that drives how their staff reacts.

"This is what creates a lot of energy in people—they feel like they're players, not spectators," Passerini said. "There's a big difference with sitting on the sidelines and waiting for the business directions. It requires different skills; it requires an agility and ability to respond. So we spent a lot of time crafting the mind-set, the skills of a successful, progressive, innovative IT professional."

■ ■ ■

They spent a lot of time crafting the exact qualities Passerini has exhibited throughout his career—though, albeit obvious, he's far more than an IT professional.

In recent years, much has been made of the *CIO-plus*, a new buzzword denoting the ascension of IT leaders to positions of greater authority and influence, often in areas that have more bottom-line impact to their companies than their original charge.

While many wear the CIO-plus badge with honor, Passerini, a CIO-plus in full, scoffs at the moniker. "To be very candid, the definition of a 'CIO-plus' is a self-fulfilling prophecy—a negative self-fulfilling prophecy," he said. "That means you are a CIO and can only aspire to be something more than that."

Passerini is one of the few sitting CIOs who is on the board of directors for a public company—in his case, United Rentals, the leading construction rental equipment provider. Passerini was elected to the board in 2009 and currently serves on three committees of the company.

And that's largely attributable to his own self-assessment: Passerini sees himself as a business leader, not a technology know-it-all. That comes from years in line management, working on various continents, and occupying a long-term seat at the executive table. Ask him about the latest buzzword technology, and he'll give you an answer you won't get from most CIOs: "I consider any technology a 'commodity,' unless we find a proven and concrete business value."

That's what separates him and other elite CIOs from the pack. "If I was thinking of myself as a technology leader, I don't think I'd be here having this conversation," he remarked during our interview.

And with that perspective comes some heady advice for the IT leaders of today. As he hears conversations at CIO conferences and reads the latest stories about the role, Passerini admits to being puzzled. There are existential questions about the future. Who am I? Where am I going? Why do I exist? Passerini said, laughingly, "I've never heard a CFO [chief financial officer] or CMO [chief marketing officer] asking themselves these questions."

Passerini's prescription for overcoming this hurdle is quite simple: Disenfranchise yourself. In more elaborate terms, forget what you know about your technology background and focus on being a businessperson—and how, as a businessperson, you can create value through technology.

It's the big picture that matters. But with it comes humility. Despite his massive influence over a company that influences our choices as consumers, he refers to his executive assistant as his "angel," invites close friends and advisors to dinner at "Chez Passerini," and, while he ticks off the most up-to-date statistics and metrics of his organization, he remains humbled even being considered among the other acclaimed IT leaders in this book.

CHAPTER 2

The Rocket Scientist: Rebecca Rhoads

A re you sitting down? the voice asked Rebecca Rhoads, who happened to be standing over her desk in Tucson, Arizona.

When she picked up the phone, Rhoads was CIO of Raytheon's electronics systems business. Raytheon's then-CEO, Dan Burnham, had other ideas.

"Well, I think you need to sit down," Burnham said, as Rhoads recounts. In that instant, she thought to herself, "What have I done?"

It was a Monday, in April 2001.

There haven't been too many times in her career when Rhoads experienced that uneasy feeling when time stands still, when everything else around you ceases to grab your attention. But this was one of them.

Burnham asked Rhoads to come up to the company's Lexington, Massachusetts, headquarters to speak with him about becoming Raytheon's next corporate CIO. As the IT leader at a multibillion-dollar Raytheon unit, she was used to moving fast. But she didn't know how fast this conversation would go.

On Wednesday, she was in Lexington. By Friday, she was the enterprise-wide CIO of Raytheon.

■ ■ ■

In 2012, Raytheon reported sales of $24 billion. It had 68,000 employees around the world, and it ranked number 117 on the Fortune 500 that year.

The company boasts a long tradition of innovation in the development of the aerospace and defense industries. When *Apollo 11* landed on the moon in 1969, it was guided by a Raytheon computer. Millions watched on TV as Neil Armstrong took the first steps on the moon's surface, thanks to Raytheon's microwave tube, which beamed TV and radio signals to Earth.

Another generation had the chance to witness Raytheon's capability in living color. During the Persian Gulf War, TV reporters talked of Iraqi Scud missiles posing a threat to Israel and Saudi Arabia. Raytheon's Patriot missiles intercepted attempted strikes at those countries and represented, according to the company, the first missile to engage another in combat.

The landmark innovations go on and on. But in the years prior to Rhoads's rise to the CIO perch, America's aerospace and defense industry had been on a wild ride of consolidation spurred by the Department of Defense. For its part, between 1995 and 1997, Raytheon spent nearly $13 billion on a handful of rival defense and aerospace businesses. These included Chrysler Corporation's defense electronics and aircraft-modification units, the defense and electronics business of Texas Instruments, and the defense and aerospace lines from Hughes Electronics, a General Motors subsidiary.

It's one thing to buy a few small competitors and integrate them into your business. However, as Rhoads noted, some of these businesses were about the same size as Raytheon itself. There were cultural differences, systems disparities, and other big-ticket merger issues. And Raytheon had to get it right: the company had gone all-in in these industries, divesting most of its nondefense holdings. These buys collectively constituted *the* big bet on the future of the company.

They were bold moves, to be sure. And the situation called for bold measures: the executive team had its hands full in devising an integration strategy—forming what Rhoads referenced as "the new Raytheon."

Still, the company faced other challenges. Not only did Raytheon rack up approximately $13 billion in debt from those deals but also investors were getting anxious waiting for a payoff from an industry that had been dramatically reshaped through mergers and acquisitions.

All of this put added pressure on Rhoads as she assumed her new role—a role that included being a key player in advancing the business of a renewed Raytheon while also fulfilling a mandate to rein in IT spending. "We were challenged after the mergers in terms of our financial performance, and we knew that landing on a dime, that is, within 10 percent, was not nearly good enough. We needed to execute with predictability and precision. We needed to land on a penny. And to do that, we needed to make a change at the front end and run IT like a business."

Two years after Rhoads took over as CIO, William H. Swanson became the company's CEO. He quickly worked to recast the company's teamwork mentality to tackle the challenges ahead. Rhoads and Swanson already had a strong relationship—she had been CIO for the unit he previously headed. That trust, paired with Rhoads's business smarts, was critical in blending with the other executives Swanson was leading into a new mode of collaboration.

How Rhoads gained and strengthened that business acumen is itself a unique story.

■ ■ ■

CIOs are certainly a rare breed. Of all C-level executives, IT leaders seem to have the most varied backgrounds. CFOs typically come with a strong financial education and work experience. CEOs have proven their worth in various business-line and strategic leadership roles, and MBAs are beyond common in those ranks.

CIOs, on the other hand, tend to have varied backgrounds. As the least mature of standard C-level roles—in terms of overall life span—there still is no secret sauce, no prototype background that will predict future success.

That said, it's hard to find a CIO with Rhoads's specific pedigree. That's because she's a rocket scientist.

In her first role in corporate America, Rhoads served as an electrical engineer for General Dynamics, designing automated test systems for the three primary missile systems of the era: standard missiles (ship-borne guided missiles), Stinger missiles (portable surface-to-air missiles), and rolling airframe missiles (infrared homing surface-to-air missiles).

She rotated through various assignments in engineering and manufacturing, design engineering, and quality systems engineering. Then came an opportunity that helped mold her thinking about business and leadership. Rhoads was chosen to lead a test systems development organization at the missiles business of Hughes Aircraft.

"We delivered test systems, and within that, we had a business model—we had manufacturing, we had matériel, we had backlog, inventory, sell-offs," she said. "We had all the components you have when you're running a business."

Rhoads also learned a few valuable lessons that would ultimately catapult her into IT leadership. In aerospace engineering, as she recounted, independent and dependent variables are clearly defined. In IT, she said, everyone is an independent variable. "You have 68,000 employees?" she asked. "That means you have 68,000 independent variables."

She also became intrigued by what she calls the "science of business"—focusing not only on how strong engineering, systems, and technical management would benefit customers but also on how they would benefit the company.

Her pathway to IT came through an event that made technology professionals far and wide cringe: Y2K. Like many CIOs across various industries at the time, Rhoads saw some measure of panic throughout the private sector—and that reaction was causing different sectors to approach the issue in different ways. But Rhoads looked at it through her engineering lens. Raytheon had deliverable software, it had business software, and it had software assets. "I was pretty vocal during the Y2K period. I said, 'Let's think this through like systems engineers.' We put together a comprehensive, integrated master plan, and started executing like we knew how to do," Rhoads said.

Rhoads pointed to that experience when she reflected on why she was chosen to lead Raytheon's IT organization. Sure, her technical background mattered, given Raytheon's business. But her test-systems leadership and contributions to Y2K—combined with an MBA from UCLA's Anderson Graduate School of Business Management—gave her the full package.

But she also understood that while those experiences prepared her to assume the CIO role, they wouldn't necessarily help her deliver on the huge integration and transformation challenges the company faced. And she also understood that technology alone—or itself—wouldn't solve the problem.

■ ■ ■

Enter Rebecca Rhoads's office at Raytheon's headquarters (which moved to Waltham, Massachusetts, in 2003), and you'll notice a few things. The first focal point is at 12 o'clock: a photo of her two grown kids as young children, smiling down at her desk. "My favorite picture," Rhoads said during an interview.

Atop cabinets that take up almost a full wall of her office sit more than a dozen framed photos of large groups: Raytheon's leadership teams through the years.

"There were challenging times, and I learned many things from them. There's no one person. There's no one strategy," Rhoads said. "Bill [Swanson] put together a team, and the team did some heavy lifting for several years. We worked it together."

Like many of the other CIOs profiled in this book, Rhoads expressed great respect for her corporate leadership team, which Swanson assembled to turn all those massive acquisitions into profits. They quickly made a decision on the IT front that would shape the next decade-plus for the company: to establish one common platform on which the whole company would run.

As Rhoads recalled, since the acquired companies were so large, Raytheon didn't have one singular IT portfolio or infrastructure to rely on. But the "new Raytheon" would have to find one, and they would have to build it together.

They started by looking at the legacy companies' enterprise resource planning [ERP] initiatives, all of which, according to Rhoads, "struggled mightily." ERP initiatives are no cakewalk. Every CIO or reader of this book knows that.

This was more complex, though. For starters, no ERP implementation is perfect—the number of CIOs and IT professionals who have struggled with it, or faced considerable setbacks or cost overruns, could fill a baseball stadium. But this project meant analyzing implementations from several large legacy businesses. Processes were not always as visible as Rhoads and her team would have liked, and the interdependencies were astounding.

Instead of starting with the technology itself, the company delved into the processes that it used across its various organizations and acquisitions. That was a decision Rhoads championed, but it wasn't complete without the support and true partnership of Raytheon's CEO and the rest of his leadership team, to whom Rhoads gives tremendous credit.

"We started with the commitment around companywide common processes," Rhoads said. "Rather than going out into the company as an IT function and selling it as the IT solution, we were all aligned from a business perspective first. That allowed the IT organization to partner with every function and every aspect—all of which were also going through transformation." All of this was taking place with the very active sponsorship of CEO Swanson, she explained.

The vision was to build a business model that was not only immediately rewarding but also enduring. The vision was to take the long view.

They started with the finance organization, which would be the test case—and the proving ground—for the company's big bet on a single, common platform.

■ ■ ■

Most people wouldn't be surprised if Raytheon had built its own platform from the ground up. The company had a long lineage of breakthroughs and innovations, so a decision to build its own ERP would be in keeping with that tradition.

But Rhoads, like so many other savvy IT leaders, took a different approach. "It's not about technology. We could have done it with any set of technologies. They're all commercially available—we don't have any exclusives on them," she said. "It's not what you use, it's how you implement it, and how you leverage technology to come together to tune your business model."

Either way, technology would be involved, but to produce results that are truly enduring, Rhoads had to make some forward-looking decisions on which technologies would be viable in the future.

When it came to finance, the corporate and divisional CFOs were committed to the overall company mission, and they also had their own vision of how they could operate more effectively. Although Rhoads admits that the first few forays were "incredibly painful," both sides knew the stakes, so they soldiered on.

Rhoads and her team grew to understand finance's vision more clearly. They delved deep into contracts management. They explored the supply base and how it would be managed. And they developed a plan for unshackling finance to meet their goals.

One noteworthy improvement that came out of that initiative positively affected the entire organization. Prior to overhauling the finance systems, it took more than 20 days to close the books. With the new improvements that Rhoads's team developed in collaboration with the finance organization, they took it down to two days. "Think about that," Rhoads said. "Now you're not spending all that time closing—you're spending that time analyzing."

That was just one example of how Rhoads's leadership helped tune a process that drove results—and on one common platform, it meant that the benefits would be realized quickly on a much broader scale.

■ ■ ■

Once they were done reengineering the finance processes, the Raytheon leadership team moved on to contracts, manufacturing, supply chain, and engineering, partnering with IT every step of the way.

Along the way, Rhoads learned an important lesson, one that every CIO working on a massive transformation needs to not only embrace but also squeeze, bear hug, and smother: what she calls "keeping it sold."

Through any long-term transformation initiative, some things are guaranteed. For one, it won't be easy. There will be roadblocks, speed bumps, and every other variety of setback. But perhaps a bigger impediment is changes to the team. Executives retire, business-unit leaders can be replaced, and the IT team itself will see inevitable turnover.

So many CIOs today talk about partnering with the business to get the support they need to push a big software purchase or a systems overhaul. But for what would be a decade-long transition for Raytheon, Rhoads knew that getting the initial go-ahead was just the start.

You also have CIOs who look at transformation as a two- to three-year program. Get in, get it done, and move on to the next thing. And too often, CIOs declare victory before victory is certain.

"When you're slogging it out, you say, 'Oh man, it would be so nice to have a two-year plan and then have that victory party,'" Rhoads said.

"Maybe it works for some companies. I tend to think that's the short game, not the long game."

But Rhoads and her colleagues at Raytheon were not in it for the short game. The real payoff, they believed, would come down the road. Sure, they could have stitched together and operated all the legacy platforms from the acquired companies. Plenty of companies do that and leave the tough decision of choosing one for another day. Making the decision to integrate the company on one platform was a bet they made early, and a bet they couldn't go back on.

That meant a constant reinforcing of the vision they had set and keeping everyone focused on the long road ahead—regardless of whether those particular leaders were there when the vision itself was born.

"You've got to be as passionate about whatever that value proposition is in year six as you were in year one," Rhoads said. "Not everyone has heard it a million times—you have. That was an 'a-ha' for us: how important it was to keep it sold, especially during the tough times."

By the fall of 2013, Rhoads was in her thirteenth year in the companywide CIO role. She and Swanson had partnered for more than 10 years, plus several years before in the business he led and she served as CIO. That collaboration has been key, Rhoads said, in helping her make an impact and continue to drive return on investment while validating the overall value proposition with her peers.

The success of the common-platform strategy has delivered benefits on many levels. "Successful internal strategies matter to the organization's key constituents—and they can become competitive differentiators," Rhoads noted. "Institutional investors gain new confidence in the company. Customers come to see us as one company. But maybe most important, they see an ongoing commitment to innovation and excellence not only in what we deliver in terms of products and services but also in the way that we run the company."

Rhoads indicated there are many different ways to measure these benefits that go far beyond traditional IT metrics. For example, Raytheon has seen significant reductions in working capital and significant improvements in cash-management practices, supplier intelligence, and other vital business processes.

Of all the overall savings and benefits to the company, only about 30 percent were IT savings. The remaining 70 percent were actually in the business itself—greater efficiencies and transformations based on the process-driven, common-platform strategy.

Along the way, over that grueling decade-plus of building the new Raytheon, Rhoads and her team reduced their IT spend as a percentage of sales by about 20 percent.

But there's one measurement she's most proud of: total shareholder return. During the interview in July 2013, she pointed to a 12-year graph mapping total shareholder return since the company began the integration. The only real dip came in 2008 to 2009, when the economy fell into a recession. Otherwise, total shareholder return—which combines share price appreciation and reinvested dividends—rose 170 percent over 12 years.

■ ■ ■

As Rhoads mentioned, the first forays were tough. Now imagine what it was like convincing not only her team but also all the organizations across the company to get on board. Yes, the vision was in place, and mandates from the CEO or board of directors are expected to be followed as gospel, but the reality is often different.

It wasn't uncommon for Rhoads to hear someone in a particular division, when told about the plan for a common platform, say something like, "That's what engineering uses. Why do we have to use that?" Those kinds of reactions can be common when new processes or systems are introduced into organizations. And as often happens, Rhoads admitted that some personnel changes had to be made.

"You need to have a team that shares your vision. But then the team has to make your vision *theirs*," Rhoads said. "And when they make your vision their vision, now you're off and running. If that's not happening, then the change isn't happening."

Still, when Rhoads was asked if the change management or culture clash was akin to a wall, she paused—but what she said next neatly embodies her leadership style and her way of viewing challenges. "I'm not sure it always looked like a wall," she said. "Maybe that's it—I just don't see it that way, so I don't approach it that way."

She went on to again stress the importance of the partnerships with senior leaders at Raytheon. She also acknowledged that her team had to do their part—to take off their techie hats and work with the businesses on their terms. Rhoads and her team could save the day on the IT front, but if they tried to do it by employing methods that clashed with the organizations they were trying to help, she knew there would be critical disconnects.

It all came back to the decision to start with process. Raytheon's team established a process that started with the requirement. And the requirement came from the customer, not IT. They would figure out the requirements, look at alternatives, and then decide whether to fund the solution.

If they were to proceed, they would continue to question, say, if the design still makes sense. Before they deploy, they do a readiness review. Then they evaluate if they have moved to a sustaining or support model.

That method, Rhoads said, is in Raytheon's DNA—she and her organization simply embraced it. And that paid off. As they continued on their journey for well over a decade, up to the present day, Raytheon outgrew or modulated its model to meet any needs along the way. But since the entire company was operating through a shared vision, everyone would be looking at where they could improve, where they could make adjustments.

Rhoads and her team weren't a siloed function. They weren't viewed as a cost center or a utility. Keeping the lights on mattered, but what mattered more was that Rhoads's IT organization had become something of a central nervous system of the growing, evolving Raytheon.

■ ■ ■

In 2013, Raytheon announced two major changes that became possible because of the dramatic changes its leadership had initiated—and that will guide the company into its next era.

In January 2013, Raytheon consolidated some operations into an organization called Global Business Services (GBS). Swanson tapped Rhoads to lead the new organization that is building on the success of the company's well-instituted enterprise efficiency initiatives by more broadly applying proven service delivery practices—beginning with the company's finance, supply chain management, HR, and IT functions. "We ask ourselves: What are additional strategies that will continue to differentiate the company?" Rhoads said. "We think the GBS operating model will give us an advantage 5 years from now, or 10 years from now."

Effective April 1, 2013, Raytheon consolidated its six businesses into four: Intelligence, Information, and Services; Integrated Defense Systems; Missile Systems; and Space and Airborne Systems. A company announcement at the time stated the move was initiated "to streamline operations, increase productivity and achieve stronger alignment with its customers' priorities." Raytheon said the consolidation will lead to $85 million in cost savings with only a modest reduction in its number of employees.

To some, those big changes could mark the climax of more than a decade of significant change at the $24 billion company. But not for Rhoads.

"We're not done." She said those words over and over when describing Raytheon's integration journey. It's a long-term continuous improvement program, but on steroids.

She ticked through some of the necessities. Enterprise-wide risk management? Check. Traditional infrastructure? Check. Internal information security controls? Check. Effective governance model? Check.

"Do we have to work through the final realignment and reconfiguring for product lines and programs? Yes," Rhoads said. "We can execute the realignment at the speed of a good decision, and it takes time to *make* a good decision. So as the four businesses are making decisions around their product lines, we're able to stay in step with them, and when they've made their business decisions, we can get everything else locked and loaded."

Raytheon is looking into a future where the common-platform strategy and constant collaboration among senior leadership will not just stay in place but continue to evolve. Rhoads pointed to the GBS organization as a case in point. She's asked senior leaders to sit on governance boards. She and her team are looking to them to champion their initiatives, but they know they need to give these leaders the right information to help them make the right decisions.

That means speaking the language of business. Speak the language of IT, and confusion clouds that decision-making process. IT professionals can kick and scream, yelling, "We know what we want to do!" But as Rhoads pointed out, that means you probably haven't listened to what the business wants you to do.

And having that constant support and interaction with executives—"staying power," as Rhoads called it—helps her and her team get it done. Those executives work with her to keep asking the hard questions. Have they outgrown their governance model? At times, the answer has been yes. Their direct involvement leads to a quicker, more effective tuning of that model when the time comes.

■ ■ ■

When Rhoads quickly relocated to Massachusetts to take the enterprise CIO role, she told herself, "Fasten your seat belt." It wasn't her inner monologue repeating the captain's orders; instead, it was her acknowledgment that the world she was stepping into would have an "insatiable appetite" for her time and abilities.

There have been a few times during her tenure as Raytheon's CIO when Rhoads thought she might be doing too much, too fast. When she posed the question to Swanson, or showed a bit of hesitancy, he provided guidance that has stuck with her.

"He'll remind you that when you're driving hard and fast, and championing change, you have to see through the curve," she said, citing one of Swanson's favorite phrases. "Don't slow down, don't lose confidence. Drive and maintain your focus on the horizon."

Keep pushing. And hope that, as a CIO, you are lucky enough to have a long-term partnership with a CEO who shares a passion for the business.

Today, when she speaks with young engineers or IT professionals, Rhoads tells them to keep their cool. Even when your position or assignment makes you uncomfortable, do not lose your confidence.

"The people who put you in that job had all the confidence in the world in you. They're asking you to take on a lot," Rhoads said. "Maybe they're stretching you in the role, but they're not losing confidence, and you just have to recognize that it's going to be difficult, it's going to be messy—the stuff in the foxhole is not what you expected, but the last thing you need to do is start to get weak-kneed and lose confidence in your ability."

She knew when she answered the call that the role would demand everything she had. And more than 13 years into the job, with more than 3,500 legacy systems retired, the rocket scientist is still accelerating.

CHAPTER 3

The Fixer: Steve Bandrowczak

The phone was ringing.

It could have been anyone. Steve Bandrowczak was only in his first week as CIO of DHL; he was constantly speaking with new colleagues and learning the terrain of the global shipping giant.

He had a budget of more than $2 billion, with 220,000 users in 220 countries. In time, Bandrowczak would come to call that job "the cocaine of the CIO role." He dined with Colin Powell. He had meetings with princes, senators, and prime ministers. He could pick up the phone and speak with Bill Gates and other top CEOs.

But this wasn't one of those calls. The voice on the other end belonged to the senior vice president of operations (SVP) at JFK International Airport in New York.

Steve:	Hello, Steve Bandrowczak.
SVP:	Are you the new CIO? I'm getting creamed out here, and I need you here as soon as possible.

The problem was simple—and complex. Before any DHL aircraft from overseas lands in the United States, the entire inventory needs to clear customs electronically. That means all the information—where it's coming from, where it's going, the weight and shape of the packages, and so on—needs to be clearly detailed. If it clears, when the plane lands (in this case, at JFK), it's cleared to go to the DHL hangar. Once inside, workers unload and sort the packages for the next step in their journey, and the plane gets ready to go back to its point of origin. That entire process can take up to four hours.

Simple. Lengthy, but simple.

But what happens if even one item doesn't clear customs? The workers have to go into the plane, find that specific item, take it out, and give it to customs. Well, if DHL's systems aren't operating correctly, the whole inventory won't clear. So take a plane with 45,000 packages, and just try to estimate the time it would take to sort them all manually. Then add in the fact that Customs—a notoriously disgruntled workforce—has to oversee that handling.

"They don't want to be doing that," Bandrowczak said. "They want to be at Dunkin' Donuts."

So Bandrowczak called his head of operations, who tells him that everything is fine. Bandrowczak—already a 10-year veteran of the CIO ranks—knows that can't be the case. He called SVP at JFK and said he'd be there at 4 A.M. the next day, when the first DHL flight was scheduled to arrive.

That morning, Bandrowczak stood with the SVP as more than 20 different flights came in. When the DHL plane arrived, the company's scanners didn't work. "So you get the visual of what happens—hundreds of people standing there with their fingers up their noses because nothing works," Bandrowczak said. "The plane is there, but the scanner doesn't work, so no packages come off."

Next stop: meeting the Customs officials at JFK. Bandrowczak walked down the hall and into the Customs office. He was greeted by a burly, brusque official who asked him point-blank, "Are you responsible for DHL's systems?" Bandrowczak answered yes. For most CIOs—or any business leader, for that matter—the next words out of the Customs official's mouth could bring to life their worst fears: "I'm shutting you down."

■ ■ ■

Steve Bandrowczak has dealt with plenty of pressure-filled situations in his 20-plus years as a chief information officer. Before arriving at DHL, he was CIO at Avnet for 10 years. In that decade, the electronics components company acquired 40 different companies—meaning Bandrowczak's team was integrating one new acquisition every quarter, on average.

Following seven years at DHL, he became CIO at Lenovo, where he oversaw the integration of IBM's personal computer business, which Lenovo acquired for $11 billion in 2005. Next came Nortel, where Bandrowczak went from CIO to head of enterprise sales. When

Avaya purchased Nortel's enterprise services unit, Bandrowczak moved with it and soon became head of its data solutions business. Finally, in mid-2012, he joined Hewlett-Packard, where he served as CIO of its Enterprise Services business. In October 2013, he was promoted to senior vice president, leading the company's Global Business Services unit.

None of it came easy, though. He was born in South Ozone Park, a Queens, New York, community situated just north of John F. Kennedy International Airport. His family—which he described as "less than wealthy"—eventually moved about 25 miles east to Copiague, New York, a diverse and largely lower-middle-class hamlet on Long Island.

He began working at age 12, and by 16, he was working 40 hours a week in a local deli. A year later, he got into heavy construction, where he would work for most of the next decade. "When you grow up in a multicultural, less affluent area, you have a lot of things that make you tougher, more resilient," Bandrowczak said.

Eventually, a friend who worked in technology told Bandrowczak about the Grumman Data Systems Institute, which offered six-month courses in operations. Bandrowczak completed the program and got a job working the graveyard shift at a local electronics company. He went back to Grumman to learn assembler code, COBOL, and FORTRAN. All the while, he worked toward his associate's and bachelor's degrees—sleeping a few hours a night—and the rest is history.

His New York upbringing proved to be priceless when solving the JFK situation. When Bandrowczak told the burly, gruff Customs official he would solve the problem in a week, the official said the CIO couldn't be from Arizona, the home of DHL's American headquarters. "I grew up in New York," Bandrowczak replied. The customs official loosened up.

It turned out DHL had a software glitch that didn't detect the failed scanner. On top of that, the RF antenna needed to be reengineered and redeployed. A week later, the problem was fixed, and DHL had no operational issues going forward. And the customs official became one of Bandrowczak's best friends.

But geography isn't everything. It was Bandrowczak's ability to visualize the problem and set firm deadlines for finding the solution that led to the positive outcome. "When you see the operations and spend time there, you get a good feel for how to fix it," he said. "The CIO needs to know the business. We talk about this a lot—but when you really get into the bowels of it, you find out how systems impact the business, how processes impact the business, how you make their life better."

All of that came into play when Bandrowczak faced an even tougher challenge at DHL—the toughest, in fact, that he faced in his entire career.

■ ■ ■

As Bandrowczak was sifting through the JFK dilemma, his company was working through its own: DHL was losing roughly $1 billion a year.

DHL, a division of Deutsche Post, grew from a one-man courier service into one of the largest international express mail businesses in the world. The company was founded in 1969 and expanded internationally until 2001, when Deutsche Post took ownership from founders Adrian Dalsey, Larry Hillblom, and Robert Lynn.

The founders—whose initials made up the company name—had built a robust international delivery business. But it had its limitations.

The company Bandrowczak arrived at was a traditional overnight air business. Top competitors FedEx and UPS had launched new offerings like ground transport and second-day delivery—at a much lower cost and with the same level of service. So instead of relying on overnight shipping, companies had new options for shipping. And they were more than happy to take advantage of the new options FedEx and UPS gave them.

"There were a variety of other services available in the industry," Bandrowczak said, "and DHL didn't have them." But they would have to, if they wanted to survive.

That was the company-wide issue; meanwhile, DHL's IT department had problems of its own.

According to Bandrowczak, when he arrived, the IT organization's delivery performance was "horrific." Systems were unstable. Networks were unstable. Seventy percent of IT projects were over budget and underdelivered.

The company's financial performance led to a lot of these problems. "IT was struggling because there was no money, so we couldn't invest," Bandrowczak said. "We couldn't get the core things done. There was no alignment with the business on priorities and projects."

And the natives were getting restless: Bandrowczak said IT personnel were demoralized following the announcement that DHL would shut down data centers and centralize them in two locations, Kuala Lumpur and Scottsdale, Arizona—a facility that was not yet built.

Despite these organizational issues, Bandrowczak had to play a leading role in launching those alternative delivery services. But the scope of the project was daunting. To get it done, Bandrowczak and his colleagues had to build new ways to pick up packages. They needed new trucks. They needed new ground transportation processes. They needed new sorting systems and new web services. "Long story short, everything needed to launch those businesses was on the backs of IT," Bandrowczak said. "But when I joined, every meeting I was in was about losing $1 billion because of IT."

■ ■ ■

Most IT organizations are very process-heavy—there's a way of doing everything from development to systems updates, and IT leaders must be masters of leading, managing, and altering those processes.

In other words, there are rules. In the most stringent organizations, those rules are gospel—break them at your own peril. But there's a flip side: As General Douglas MacArthur once said, "Rules are mostly made to be broken and are too often for the lazy to hide behind."

Bandrowczak is anything but lazy. He's run a marathon. He mentors students in Columbia University's Executive Masters in IT Management program and military veterans in Workforce Opportunity Services' IT training programs. He routinely starts his day at 4:30 A.M.

And while he sees the importance of processes and controls, he had a $1 billion problem staring him straight in the face.

Bandrowczak quickly realized that he couldn't lead the launch with the team he had in place. So he got together with Randy Clark, the head of sales, and Fred Beljaars, who ran operations, to strategize a plan. All three faced the same organizational problems. All three had seen the same obstacles in standing up the new business offerings.

So they decided to break all the rules.

Bandrowczak pulled the best people from his IT team—pulling from every process and skill set, from systems development life cycle (SDLC) to design—and created, in his words, a rogue organization. "Everybody on that team was dreaded and hated because they were breaking every rule. They were outside the norm, outside the organization, outside of normal processes," Bandrowczak said. "It was a rogue organization—and I empowered them to be a rogue organization. Break every rule—I don't care. We have to get this done. Whatever it takes, we'll do it."

Clark and Beljaars did the same, and the entire group was called into a conference room and given a critical—and monumental—first objective: Come back in a week and tell the executives how they could launch ground and second-day businesses in 90 days. According to Bandrowczak, everything was on the table. Whatever they needed to spend, they could. If they needed more resources, no problem. New systems? Go for it. But one thing was nonnegotiable: the 90-day time frame.

A lot happens every 90 days. Public companies file quarterly statements. Seasons change. People get a little older.

For Bandrowczak and his executive peers, making the call wasn't easy. Their teams had never been through such a detailed and arduous project, so they literally didn't know their own capabilities.

But they didn't have a choice.

In that room in Scottsdale, Project Terra was born. They were betting the farm.

■ ■ ■

The term *burning platform* has become a fixture in the lexicon of organizational change and change management. It couldn't have been more relevant to what DHL was experiencing—and the challenge Bandrowczak and his team were undertaking.

Setting the 90-day timeline was a tough call, for many reasons. And the ramifications and reverberations were equally tough to stomach.

The announcement would get widespread publicity. If that story lands on the cover of the *Wall Street Journal*, you had better believe another story will be written 90 days later. And if DHL didn't succeed in meeting that goal, that story wouldn't be pretty. And beyond the public relations disaster that would ensue, the financial markets would react—negatively, to be sure.

And if they had hit the 90-day mark with a subpar offering, the fallout could have been equally disastrous. Factor in the very real notion that UPS and FedEx were just waiting for DHL to fail so they could scoop up disenchanted clientele, and you have the crystal-clear denotation of "betting the farm."

DHL already had ground and second-day businesses in Europe, but Bandrowczak and his team were starting from scratch. In Europe, there was complexity in transportation laws and policies from country to country. In the United States, they had to deal with NAFTA—cross-Canada, cross-Mexico, cross-America, cross-continental. In the end, the new U.S. offerings would be more than 80 percent new to DHL.

There would undoubtedly be plenty of IT-centric issues. For example, DHL's IT organization had been doing 45-day user-acceptance testing. They were 90 days to launch, so they had to winnow that process down to two weeks. An even more daunting prospect: they would have to load new software onto 40,000 scanners and test them—in a weekend.

Bandrowczak had doubts about his team before launching Project Terra, but now he was seeing the harsh reality of the painstaking time frame. "It got to be a whole series of creating pain for the organization," Bandrowczak said. "This is a team that couldn't keep 10-year-old applications at 60 percent availability."

While reviewing initial plans for processes and procedures in Project Terra, Bandrowczak's team was telling him something he absolutely dreads: "We can't." Whatever was being discussed, he kept hearing "we can't."

If you know Bandrowczak, you know he's a rather no-nonsense executive. His response: "That's not what I asked. Tell me the trade-offs we need. What is the art of the possible?"

■ ■ ■

Shortly before Bandrowczak joined DHL, Ron Kifer came on board to start up a new program management office. Just like IT needed a major overhaul, DHL had no coherent project management office (PMO) strategy. Although the entire organization was insourced, it lacked the professional program and project portfolio management discipline you would expect at such a large, global company. At the time of his arrival, Kifer says the company's project delivery success rate was somewhere around 40 percent.

But the company couldn't wait: Kifer and Bandrowczak had to build their capabilities in parallel with Project Terra. Along with rolling out the new business, they also had to contend with building out the Scottsdale data "supercenter," as Kifer called it, as well as moving the corporate headquarters from downtown San Francisco to Plantation, Florida. Along the way, too, they would be tasked with integrating Airborne Express, which DHL purchased to bolster the ground-business operation.

"It was the most intense, large-scale enterprise transformation initiative I've been involved in, and I've been involved in a lot of them over a 40-year career," Kifer said.

The immediate priority was building the necessary delivery engine. They established an enterprise managed services model, moving low-value activities to partners so they could focus internally on critical, high-value initiatives. And they retained an army of recruiters to bring in top talent, leading to hundreds of new hires in the initial stages of Project Terra.

This was all being done in the shadow of a rather complex corporate culture. Kifer called it one of the most aggressive cultures he's ever operated in. The most unique quality was DHL's perspective on change. Although most large organizations resist change, DHL's appetite for change was so voracious that many functional organizations struggled to keep up. For Kifer and Bandrowczak, it was about getting ahead of the curve.

Despite the tumultuous tasks they faced, Bandrowczak and Kifer can't point to any specific crisis that could have doomed Project

Terra. As Kifer recalled, the biggest hurdles came from afar—it was business-side planning and execution that caused the most headaches. Take the new sortation facility the company set up in Cincinnati. The IT and project teams installed all the technological capabilities needed for their new sorting requirements, but the business staffed the facility with contract workers who were poorly trained and ill-prepared for the volume they would be handling. Packages were delayed for days as the company tried to fix the problem.

"We had warned about these issues going into Day One activities without much success," Kifer said. "Watching it blow up and not being able to do anything about it—that was pretty tough, especially after we had been so successful on the IT side."

■ ■ ■

Having the right people in the right place at the right time is critical to any project success. It's never perfect, and plenty of changes happen in the trenches of a project. But the human factors can't be ignored—not only do you need the right people, but you need the right leader.

"Steve is clearly a maverick in terms of aggressively driving agendas," said Kifer, who came out of retirement after serving as CIO of Applied Materials to join Bandrowczak as vice president for global IT at HP. "He's a friend to process and methodology, but he's the first guy to go around it to get things done and achieve a business outcome. But in parallel with that, he has his teams working on the business process reengineering to solve the problem long term. Steve gets results because he doesn't allow bureaucracy and policy to prevent achieving business outcomes he's committed to."

Bandrowczak attributes much of his leadership style and strategic perspective to the lessons he learned from Project Terra. He zeroes in on two breakthrough revelations in particular: having a vision and how you actually envision overseeing major projects.

"The first thing is, good leaders have an endless amount of energy to drive others' energy," he said. "They have a complex set of tasks but can boil them down into a simple *vision*." Having a vision is essential for successful leadership—even if the leader downplays the idea initially. President George H. W. Bush—widely praised as one of the more intellectual foreign policy thinkers in modern presidential history—played down the idea during his first campaign for the presidency. When a friend urged him to go on a retreat to solidify his governing strategy, President Bush was widely quoted as responding with frustration, "Oh, the vision thing."

Bandrowczak admits that setting a clear, comprehensive vision is no easy task. No one can predict the future, no matter how much information sits in front of you. But when you have no answers, no predictions, leaders must set a course that aims their teams at arriving at an optimal result. "If you create the right vision, simplify it so people understand it, and put energy around it, people will find a way to get it done," Bandrowczak said. "That's a commonality in my leadership style. At HP, we have a lot of things that I don't know how the hell we'll get done, but you create a vision and atmosphere for people to be successful, and magical things will happen."

When it comes to project leadership, too many executives make the same mistake: they think that a rigorous PMO policy will best limit risk and ensure successful delivery. But just like setting a vision, charting this course is not simple. Every project has its own intricacies. Different business partners want projects to run a certain way. And those partners often have very different definitions of process and success.

For IT leaders, it's all about adapting to those different requirements and demands. Bandrowczak has made a career of tackling enormous challenges at very different companies, and he cites the ability to adapt as one of the most critical skills a leader must possess. "Sometimes you need a Patton that runs over everything. Sometimes you need someone to play Gandhi and harmonize everyone together," he said. "Every project is very different. There's no one formula for making them successful. What's common are the individuals who know how to motivate, create energy, create that end vision, and make sure everyone plays their part."

But you can't ignore the fact that those lessons were also forged out of necessity—on DHL's burning platform. Although he admits that maybe some companies wouldn't have taken such bold action had they not had such a financial disaster on their hands, he also sees a flip side to that thinking. "Good companies always have that healthy paranoia," he said. "A lot of companies don't. You see a lot of great things come out of necessity as opposed to a normal course of action."

Bandrowczak and his colleagues weren't gauging success based on getting a particular system in place or securing business from a particular partner. The latter is an aftereffect; the former is just one milestone among many. The bottom line for Project Terra was the bottom line for DHL: the measurement of success was avoiding all-out failure and driving new profitability into a then-rebuilding business.

The team did their best to make all appropriate trade-offs to make the project work. They weren't concerned with getting everything right—if they could get 70 percent on the mark, they could will themselves through the remaining 30 percent.

"I've always maintained that one of the key characteristics of great change leaders is the courage to do the tough things, even when it doesn't work to your advantage," Kifer said. "Steve has that—I learned that from him, and it's part of my MO having had the opportunity to work with him."

It goes back to vision: In Bandrowczak's view, bringing everyone together with a shared goal—saving the business—drives success and productivity far more than operating such a huge initiative in silos. "You've been to hell together, but you had each other's backs," he said. "Everyone will be on that burning platform, and the only chance of survival is if we all link arms and climb down together."

■ ■ ■

That sense of necessity drove him in his subsequent leadership roles, continuing today as head of HP's Global Business Services. In the end, Bandrowczak made a realization that is critical to any CIO facing a steep challenge in which IT can truly be a game-changer: "The science of IT is less important than partnering with the business to come up with the art of IT."

Driving that motivation requires many things of a leader. Beyond the vision, a CIO in that scenario needs to inspire a high level of dedication, focus, and energy. But the leader needs to be his or her own follower—if the CIO is lacking in those areas, it trickles down.

So then comes the question: Who are the right people to handle these responsibilities? When running up against necessity—think about it, once again, as a bet-the-farm proposition—a leader also needs to keep close tabs on the temperature in that boiler room. People burn out. People get frustrated. In the midst of all the pressure, some people can forget what they're working toward.

Bandrowczak harkened back to his time at Avnet, when his IT organization was a veritable integration machine, taking in 40 new acquisitions in 10 years. "The reality is, you never know what kind of people can get through projects like that until you do it," Bandrowczak says. "You don't know until you know."

Although some companies offer laser-focused profiles of the type of talent they require, Bandrowczak doesn't believe there's a coherent formula for finding the people who can thrive in the most pressure-filled situations. "Everybody wants to be successful," he said. "Nobody's DNA makes them come to work and say, 'I want to be a loser today.' And everybody likes being on teams, but it's only a certain amount of people who can drive that energy, that passion it takes to move a program. So it's about those people who can keep the burning platform and keep the goal line in front of them."

■ ■ ■

Back to vision. Bandrowczak has a saying—really, more of an operating doctrine—that he uses with his team at HP: "I don't want to crawl to mediocrity—I want to run to greatness."

Plenty of corporate leaders, coaches, consultants, and academics like to use little sayings or clichés as an allusion to their business philosophies. But it's not every day that one follows a statement like that with real, substantive examples.

Enter Bandrowczak. He's been known to cite metrics and statistics from his past businesses with precision, and he can quickly analyze what he sees in his competitive playing field—which comes in handy, particularly when you're playing to win.

Let's say he wanted to implement a new material requirements planning (MRP) system. Most companies will say their aim is to get their supply chain from 10 turns on inventory to 12 or even 15. Bandrowczak asks, "What is the best in the industry?"

As he explains, if his team is the best, it makes a serious impact on his profit and loss. If they're the best, they can translate those faster cycle times to real dollars. When you see real dollars, you see real potential impact. No abstract thinking here—Bandrowczak doesn't have much tolerance for wishy-washy, theoretical ideas.

So say he can increase inventory turns by five, which results in projected annual returns of $100 million. Many would be happy to sit back and wait for the money to come rolling in. Instead, Bandrowczak reasserts that sense of necessity: "I say to my team, 'Who is going to write a check for $100 million that I'm losing because we can't get a system up?'" That's the bluntness of his approach.

In his eyes, being the best isn't just something to brag about. It's a goal that he doesn't see as unrealistic—but that he feels too few CIOs actually recognize. "We challenge ourselves with how to be great, how to be best in the industry," Bandrowczak said. "Any PMO will give you good clear goals for business outcomes. But you say, is that best in class? Is that best in the industry? Are you the middle of the pack, or whale crap in the ocean? They'll say, 'I don't know, but I know I'm 5 percent better than I was last year.'"

And he reasserts his intolerance for mediocrity every chance he gets. Every day he tells his team they need to be better than their competitors. If they stack themselves up against the competition—in everything from quoting cycle times to receivables to capital returns—and see that they're lacking, as Bandrowczak says, a change opportunity presents itself. And if they can master those areas and beat the other industry players, his team gets better by default.

Bandrowczak also takes issue with CIOs and business leaders griping about the difficulties in prioritizing key projects. For him, it comes back to a few simple elements: the right portfolio, the right staff, and the right resources. If you don't have those things—or can't figure out how to understand them or access them—you're in trouble.

As of January 2013, Bandrowczak's Enterprise Services IT organization was running programs that drove millions out of the P&L each month. "So if someone comes to me and says they want a blue screen,

I say if it's more than a million a month, we'll talk about it—if it's not, get to the back of the line," he says. "It's an easy conversation."

■ ■ ■

In his 20-plus years as an IT and business leader, Bandrowczak has seen plenty of changes to the role. In that time, the ideal profile of a CIO has swung back and forth like a pendulum. When the role first emerged, corporate leaders saw value in installing seasoned business professionals to run the operation. But too many lacked core under-standing of technology itself, and the function was rendered to utility status. Then came the era of the ultra-tech-savvy CIO—seasoned in IT, but not so much in business. A language barrier emerged; business leaders were looking to IT to drive cost savings and innovation, but too many of these New Age IT leaders were overly enthralled with the bits and bytes, not the dollars and cents.

In more recent years, a new hybrid profile has emerged. These new IT leaders are multilingual—comfortable in speaking the language of business to their C-suite colleagues and board, as well as the language of technology with their teams.

The days of being relegated to driving nice-to-have IT initiatives or managing a utility are long gone—at least for companies sharp enough to realize IT's value-driving potential. For those CIOs—Bandrowczak clearly being a member of that echelon—it's about transforming the business.

"The transformation of CIOs over the last five years has accelerated faster than anything we could have dreamed of when I started in this industry. And I think it's going to get even faster," Bandrowczak said. "The amount of things we need to keep up with today—not just on the technical side, but on the consumer side, how to drive revenue, how to drive a sales team, how to reinvent supply chains, the financial aspects of understanding return on capital, return on working inventory—these are things we never dreamed of, and now they're part of our DNA and our daily language. It's a dramatic shift. And it's put CIOs in a new light, a whole new position, as it relates to the success of companies."

But for the very best of the best, the technology-speak matters very little. It's about creating value—and understanding that IT has a unique perch for doing so. "IT is the only part of the company that has a natural view of opportunity to cash," Bandrowczak said. "It's the only group that can look at the interaction of how a sales team impacts downstream operations. When I launch a product, my product team is looking at getting a product out. But no one's looking at how it impacts sales, billing, shipping, supply chain, etc. In the IT community, we're the only ones who have the end-to-end view of that."

But he admits that it's still quite a shift in thinking. "Running five nines on a server is meaningless unless I hit my P&L numbers," Bandrowczak said. "Talk about operational metrics? I don't care. SLAs and uptime are unimportant if they don't drive a business outcome."

■ ■ ■

In December 2012, on a brisk Saturday morning, Bandrowczak trudged across the snow-covered campus of Columbia University to help judge thesis defenses from students in Columbia's Executive Masters in IT Management program. These master's candidates work with a CIO mentor to shape and perfect their thesis projects, and at the end of each semester, they defend them in front of a panel of CIOs and faculty members.

Student after student presented to Bandrowczak's panel, as he leaned forward, listening intently and taking notes. When the time came for comments and questions, he offered encouraging words—peppered with incredibly granular industry metrics, financial statistics, and opinions on best practices, each tailored for each specific thesis project.

The sheer scope of Bandrowczak's knowledge was overwhelming to most of the students, but not surprising to anyone who knows him.

What might be surprising to learn—even for those who know him well—about this longtime veteran of the business and IT leadership ranks is that he's an introvert. "Not many people who've run sales are introverts," Bandrowczak said. "And I'm not a middle-of-the-road introvert—I'm a far-left introvert."

Learning that about himself led him down another path: a constant desire to improve. For example, early in his management career, he realized he was "horrific" at making presentations. So he looked for ways to practice. He went to speak at high schools and then colleges.

Next came smaller groups inside his IT organization. "There wasn't necessarily any calculated strategy to work on it," he said. "I just knew I sucked at it and had to improve." Not too many years later, he was delivering keynote speeches at the Interop trade show in front of crowds of 3,000 people.

Bandrowczak likes to work at other things, often blocking out 30 minutes or so a day to learn and improve, be it basketball, running, reading, or whatever. He sees tangible benefits; but he's disappointed that many others don't.

"I don't think people look at their careers and professions and have a conscious effort about training themselves and improving themselves," Bandrowczak said. "So if you're a CIO and you don't know what it means to build a sales funnel or close a sales funnel, go spend time with the sales team, go live in the field for a while. If you don't know what it's like to run a receivables team, go see what it's like when you have customers screaming at you and the collections desk is getting pounded."

Another important thing to know about Bandrowczak is that family—his wife, Donna, and daughter, Maree—comes first. And once, when it didn't, he had to make yet another difficult decision.

Four and a half years into his tenure at DHL, the role became too much to handle. Bandrowczak was one of the highest paid IT leaders in the country, and it's not every day you rub elbows with world leaders. But it all came with a cost. "I found myself, after years of putting everything I had into the role, that I had been to only one of my daughter's basketball games, one of her softball games," he said. "I missed so many things."

Despite generous overtures from company leadership, Bandrowczak didn't believe he could stay on. The work-life balance tilted too far in the wrong direction, and he decided to pack it up. He moved over to Lenovo, leaving stock options on the table and taking a severe pay cut. But he has no regrets. "People get hung up in this, and they destroy families without even realizing it—it's hard to see," Bandrowczak said. "I had a great home and a great car and all, but it doesn't make up for time. It's a hard balance."

But things worked out. Sitting next to him at Columbia on that frosty morning, closely analyzing the thesis defenses, was his daughter, on the verge of graduating from college, learning a few lessons from her dad.

CHAPTER 4

The Pilot: Carol Zierhoffer

t looked like the Declaration of Independence. On a large poster board, with a backdrop design that would make the Founding Fathers proud, Carol Zierhoffer laid out 10 operating principles that would guide the massive transformation of ITT.

On February 27, 2009, at a top 50 IT Leadership offsite meeting in Southern California, Zierhoffer, ITT's global CIO, put her John Hancock on the board. The company's CEO, Steve Loranger, had just delivered an impassioned endorsement of Zierhoffer's plan and principles and told the rest of the executives gathered in the room that it was their decision whether to also sign the board, but they had to decide before they left that day. And they did.

At the time, ITT was a conglomerate with two major businesses: defense and aerospace, and highly engineered industrial products with a focus on water. Internally, those businesses were made up of smaller units called value centers. They were fiercely independent of each other—they had their own leadership, including divisional CIOs, and they didn't exactly play nice with some of the centralized functions, including IT.

That was about to change. Zierhoffer and her team had set out to unify business processes and systems and to drive shared services and best practices. They would bolster information security, enable global collaboration, optimize service delivery, and completely transform the enterprise resource planning system.

And they had made great progress throughout 2009 and 2010, when, in mid-December, Zierhoffer's phone rang. On the other end was Loranger, who asked his CIO to come to his office.

Everything that was about to change was about to change again.

Zierhoffer sat down, joined by the heads of the defense and water businesses. Loranger looked them all in the eye and delivered news that no one saw coming: "We've decided to split the company into three separate publicly traded companies instead of the path that we're on," he said, as Zierhoffer recalled. "We're going to announce that publicly on January 12.

"You are now under nondisclosure. You can't talk about it, but be prepared."

Founded in 1920 as International Telephone and Telegraph, ITT had grown into a sprawling jumble of companies. During the 1960s, the company acquired such diverse concerns as Avis Rent-a-Car, the Hartford Insurance Company, Sheraton Hotels, and Continental Bakery, the maker of Wonder Bread.

The following decade, it began divesting many of its acquisitions. As time went on, Wall Street began frowning at some of these far-flung conglomerates. In 1995, ITT pared itself down to the three and then the two major operating units it boasted in 2010.

Investors applauded the announcement, sending ITT's share price up more than 16 percent. Zierhoffer, on the other hand, had what she called an "Oh, shit" moment.

Already in the process of completing the centralization process, she'd have to figure out another plan: how to reverse the plan she already put in place and get the company ready to fracture by October 2011. Think about it this way: she was speeding down the road and then had to turn 180 degrees on a dime, and the path was anything but clear.

Worse off, she had to do it alone.

■ ■ ■

Carol Zierhoffer studied nursing at the University of New Hampshire. All the women in her family were either teachers or nurses, and they influenced her to pursue that course. "Back then, that's what women did," Zierhoffer said. "You were either a teacher or a nurse." Two and a half years into her education, she entered the clinical phase and realized she hated it. She changed her minor to her major and graduated with a bachelor's degree in business administration from the university's Whittemore School of Business & Economics.

Zierhoffer began her career at Northrop Grumman, where she rose to become CIO of the company's electronic systems, IT sector, and mission systems businesses. In late 2007, her mentor, Tom Shelman, was promoted from global CIO to head Northrop's IT Defense group. She hoped the overall CIO job was open, since Shelman had been preparing Zierhoffer to succeed him.

But as Shelman departed, company leadership decided to turn the CIO role into a rotational opportunity for executives outside of IT. The first executive came into the role, and Zierhoffer put her head down and showed him the ropes. When word came out that they would rotate him elsewhere and were prepared to bring in another executive to oversee IT, Zierhoffer had another one of those moments: after almost two decades with the company, she would never get the job she wanted.

"If I really wanted to be a corporate CIO, I'd have to go do it somewhere else," Zierhoffer said. "I'll never get a 25-year pin. I'll never get a 25-year watch. But that's okay."

Before she knew it, ITT came calling. They first asked Zierhoffer to join as CIO of its defense business, which at the time was about a $6 billion unit. She spoke with them but quickly decided that she wouldn't take the offer: her Northrop Grumman division was bigger, so thanks, but no thanks.

Three months later, ITT rang again. They acknowledged that the role they offered her was too small. ITT was in the process of removing their global CIO—ironically, Zierhoffer's interviewer—and they wanted her to take over.

It was a perfect fit, she thought. She had the aerospace and defense background, which helped her bring instant credibility to the new role. But ITT was a diverse company, so the consolidating role also offered her the chance to go beyond her background and gain global commercial experience. All the while, the challenges were the same: people, processes, synergy, enabling the business, and so on.

Zierhoffer flew to White Plains and interviewed with the CEO, the CFO, the head of HR, and two board members. In October 2008, she was named global CIO.

Right away, she saw some of the dysfunction around the value center structure. When she proposed email systems across the units, one of the divisional CIOs got huffy. "*My value center president* will never allow those email servers to leave my campus," Zierhoffer heard. Why not? she asked. "*My value center president. . . .*" Zierhoffer cut her off. "I said, 'If your value center president gives a hoot about where the servers are, it's only because you've made him care where the servers are. He shouldn't care. He should only care that you're delivering to him the best, more reliable, most cost-effective email service. So why would he care where hardware sits?'" The CIO just stood there, with a blank stare.

There was a new sheriff in town, and Zierhoffer was determined to break the "me, my, mine" attitude she saw across the companies.

■ ■ ■

That disparate culture led Zierhoffer to develop her 10 principles, a clear set of guidelines around business architecture, shared services, common process, governance, accountability, information, consistency, investment, behaviors, and funding.

"You've got to get people behind what it is you're going to do, who you're going to be, and how you're going to act. You have to set a standard," Zierhoffer said during an August 2013 interview near her home in Annapolis, Maryland, where she still has the "Declaration" poster board.

She explained her leadership style as being heavily influenced by her program management and execution experience. Equally important is the notion of bringing together a team behind a shared vision. Doing that requires a personal touch.

As Zierhoffer was rising up the ranks at Northrop Grumman, then-CIO Tom Shelman launched a mentoring program. Out of 4,000 or so IT professionals at the company, 8 were selected to work personally with Shelman.

She flew to Dallas for her first meeting, prepared to talk strategies and goals for her organization. When she walked into Shelman's office, he immediately asked about her kids. How old were they? What did they like to do? That conversation lasted about 45 minutes.

Zierhoffer came to understand that leadership is very personal. If you want to form a great team—and keep it great—you have to know a lot about the people on it. "You make decisions about whom you want in your foxhole with you because you are going to go into battles together, and you've got to be willing to cover each other and have each other's back," she said. "Knowing a little bit about each other that is personal, sometimes you might be a little kinder, a little more understanding when something's not going right."

You learn their strengths and weaknesses as well, she said, and that helps you form a great team. To her, it's simple: If you're unified as a team, you'll get results. If you're not, you won't.

At ITT, Zierhoffer felt she had the right team in place. They were living the principles she established, and they were well on their way to making her transformation plan a reality.

When Loranger told her about the planned split, she had to restrategize. First, she had to determine which initiatives to stop and which to continue. But she was in a tight circle of trust around the confidential plan.

Zierhoffer quickly realized that to keep her team together, she needed help. She convinced Loranger to let her bring one more person under the tent to help formulate a plan. That would be Steve Little, her trusted deputy, who was leading the infrastructure piece of the program. (Little had been at Schneider Electric for 20 years, the past 7 as CIO, and he had decided in June 2009 to step down at the end of the year. A neighbor serendipitously connected him to Zierhoffer. They spoke for two hours on a Friday in July. That call ended with Zierhoffer asking Little to start on Monday.)

Little had created the global infrastructure organization. The shared services organization was coming along rapidly. They were preparing to announce a massive IT reorganization in January 2010, breaking up the value center model—the official communication had already been approved. The team was ready to pull the trigger on putting all employees into the central IT organization and on a common payroll system on January 3.

In other words, time was not on their side. When Zierhoffer called Little to tell him that she wanted to delay the service delivery transition, he thought she was crazy. At the time, she couldn't tell him why.

After Zierhoffer got the authorization to clue him in, she told Little the bombshell. They spent the week between Christmas and New Year's working on the new plan. Two people in the foxhole, starting a nine-month, 24/7 effort to reorganize the reorganization.

"We often joked that the project was like having triplets in nine months. And one of our ground rules was that we wanted three healthy babies—not two healthy and one anemic or weak," Zierhoffer said. "All had to be strong. And I wanted to put my fingerprints on those three being healthy."

Zierhoffer was thrilled to have Little at her side, but she also knew they'd need more help.

They sought out a consulting partner to help them push through. They called in five leading providers for three-hour, confidential briefing sessions. Zierhoffer and Little opted for Deloitte, which she said had the right experience, framework, and model, and the cultural fit was an added bonus.

Zierhoffer also reached out to peers in IT leadership who had been through similar experiences. She called senior IT executives at companies like Motorola, Cardinal Health, and Altria. What they told her would influence many of the crucial decisions she would make during ITT's triplet pregnancy.

The first lesson centered on people. Zierhoffer's executive peers told her the journey would be incredible—not just for her, but for the team. After all, how many people ever get a chance to be involved with something like this? Sell the journey, they told her—make the journey attractive to them. Incentivize them to stay. Explain what's in it for them and where they'll land. If she didn't know where that would be, just be honest with them.

That advice echoed in Zierhoffer's head; it went right back to the people-first mentality she learned at Northrop Grumman. So as she started formulating her strategy, she put her people first—win the hearts and minds of the team to get this done, and then those people would have the confidence to move forward to their new roles, wherever they might be.

■ ■ ■

Zierhoffer and Little started drawing lines about which activities would continue and which would have to stop. They couldn't disclose the full story of why, but they also weren't going to lie.

When they decided to stop the service-delivery optimization piece and the transitioning of the IT organizations into one team, they had a reason. Because they would be shifting people together from the defense and commercial businesses, ITT would need to get clearance from the government about the cost shifts. "We just want to make sure that everything was okay from a disclosure position," the explanation went. "Let's just wait. . . . We're only delaying it a month—we're not stopping it."

On the other hand, they decided to plow ahead with the global collaboration solution, which was based on SharePoint. That was a no-brainer because they knew that once they finished it, they could just clone it for the three new companies. Likewise, the teams kept moving ahead with information security, which Zierhoffer said was essential and nonnegotiable.

They also decided to speed up the ERP blueprint completion, which she and her team labeled "Program BEST," short for Business-Enabled Strategic Transformation. They needed to have that "signed, sealed, delivered, and done," Zierhoffer said, ahead of the separation announcement. That way, the new companies could leverage if they chose. The program management office running the ERP program was a "machine," she said. Once they were done, they shifted that team to the corporate breakup activities. Cindy Hoots had lead Program BEST and would transition to lead the Separation Management Office for IT and Financial Shared Services, under Zierhoffer's leadership.

Perhaps most important, they decided to hustle to finalize and sign off on the common blueprint, which encapsulated the common processes across the company and shared services.

The infrastructure separation—active directory, shared applications, one global network—was a bit more complex. Zierhoffer's industry peers gave her some insight into that activity that made it sound only more daunting.

They told Zierhoffer to expect her cost to achieve the separation to be somewhere between 20 and 40 percent of the annual IT spend, non-recurring. After that, expect your recurring run-rate to be 10 to 30 percent higher on day one. You could work that down, but each of the three companies is likely to face a 10 to 30 percent spike in the short term.

Management wasn't happy to hear that, but they also trusted the intelligence Zierhoffer had gathered. They told the CIO and her team to move forward but reminded them of the cost pressure they all faced.

That's important to any company and any IT organization, especially in a major initiative like this. But there was another twist. One of ITT's board members, Christina Gold, ran First Data when it spun out Western Union in 2006. The good news: she connected Zierhoffer with two of the executives who led that split for her. The bad news: she saw IT as a highly complex work stream in the spin-off and, if they failed, it could cause incredible damage to the breakup effort.

In essence, Gold was right—at the very least, on the last part. And it foreshadowed other doubts to come.

Zierhoffer presented her plan for separating the network and applications and everything else. Management was leery. Some questioned if Zierhoffer's team could really pull it off. Others questioned the idea of splitting the email system across the three companies.

There was another thing the executive peers warned her about. For every CIO, there are five non-IT executives with a great IT-related idea—and it probably came from the last airline magazine they read. Split the email system? "Why not just take it to the cloud? Heck, let's just transition to Gmail," Zierhoffer recalled hearing. "We had more 'great ideas' that came from airline magazines."

As comical as those may be, every CIO faces them. But in an initiative with endless twists, there would be another. And that one could have derailed Zierhoffer's efforts (yet again)—and potentially render them worthless.

■ ■ ■

There was another member of ITT's board, Linda Sanford, a longtime IBM executive, who connected Zierhoffer with their merger and acquisition (M&A) team for insight and lessons learned.

At the same time, IBM's M&A and divestiture team contacted Steve Loranger, ITT's chief, and offered a proposition. Why have Carol and her team lead the breakup? IBM could handle the whole thing and run it in an outsourced environment—and they wouldn't charge a dime for the upfront work.

Loranger approached Zierhoffer with the proposition. He thought it sounded great. She thought otherwise. "I said, 'Steve, think about how long it takes to even write an outsourcing statement of work for the complexity we have in this company today,'" Zierhoffer recalled. "Never mind splitting it at the same time. It would take you 12 to 18 months *just* to write the statement of work."

To make sure she wasn't reacting too quickly, she had already contacted her former colleague at Northrop Grumman who ran their IT outsourcing business. He confirmed for her the time frame expectation. Loranger said it couldn't be that long. Zierhoffer held firm—and prevailed.

She had a plan, a price tag, and a schedule, and she was asking for capital. But management remained wary and questioned the cost. So Zierhoffer pulled out another trick from her extensive experience in defense: form a red team.

Red teams are a convention not only of corporations but also of the military and intelligence communities. In essence, they're a backup team, independent of the team conceiving a plan, that serves as a check. Their mission is to question the solutions that team is offering. Think of it as a separate quality assurance team that tries to break and find holes in a software application the programming team has developed.

Zierhoffer urged the CEO and management committee to bring in an independent body to review the plan she put in place. She said she'd "value and welcome their input"—and she didn't care whom they picked. Zierhoffer knew she was putting the whole plan on the line, but once again, she had confidence in the team she built and the plan they had established.

Zierhoffer worked with the management committee to form the red team. They chose one of the CTOs from the aerospace and defense businesses, Chuck Eklund, as the head; a CFO from the largest commercial businesses; an executive from Bayer, who had overseen a major divestiture; two outsourcing experts from Technology Partners International (TPI), since the outsourcing option was still on the table; and an independent advisor from Deloitte's M&A practice.

Her primary team wasn't thrilled. They didn't have time for this, they screamed. Zierhoffer told them they had the time and they had the plan. The key was that this was happening—if the red team wanted to see something, the team would show them. No questions asked, no detail left unattended—and no doubts should linger in the team's mind that they had set the right course. If the red team found holes, the primary team would work to plug them. If the red team confirmed our plans, the primary team would be affirmed to move out.

The red team came to the dedicated team space in Hanover, Maryland, which had been built out just a year before to house the BEST team. The team presented the entire plan—every work stream, every level of planning and strategy—and they spent almost four days reviewing it. Her plan, in its entirety, was an open book.

When they wrapped up the review, Eklund, the red-team leader, made up his mind.

As Zierhoffer recounted, he went to the executive committee and sang the praises of the overall plan. His message was clear: the team has developed an incredible amount of disciplined process work. The level of detail and dedication was commendable. Sure, there were risks, but none that couldn't be managed with proper support from you, the management.

The plan made sense. "It's time to fish," he told them, and by the way, "you need to get out of their way and let them execute. And you need to support them. They need to hear this loud and clear from you."

■ ■ ■

Helmuth von Moltke the Elder, chief of staff to the Prussian Army in the late nineteenth century, was the originator of the ubiquitously cited quote, "No plan survives first contact with the enemy." Zierhoffer also knew this and quoted it to her team. "We knew we had a plan," she said, "but it would change as more facts unfolded."

She was dodging bullets not only from her management on her strategy and from outside parties "who wanted to help" but also from getting beyond the view of the short term (finishing the split) to the long term (what happens afterward).

Along the way, Zierhoffer and her team learned new things and adjusted their plans. That rattled some on the team, but for most, it was what they signed up for.

When Zierhoffer and her team prepared to split ITT's network, she took yet another lesson from the industry peers she consulted. Those executives—the Motorola leader, in particular—told her not to wait until the split to actually parse it. Motorola split its network on day one of its breakup and faced fallout as the company separated. (Keep in mind, as Little said, Motorola spun off the mobile business in 18 or so months, with a few years of planning, whereas ITT was spinning out three companies in 9 months.)

Zierhoffer and her team took that to heart. But with all the pressure across the board to get the separation right, when it came to the network, ITT management had a simple question: Did they have a backup plan? They'd have to have a contingency for an initiative this critical. "Yeah, yeah, we have a backup plan. Absolutely," they told them.

Truth be told, she and Little planned to fight their way through any issues. "We'd prepare and test and prepare and test and do it again," Zierhoffer said. "But there is a point of no return with some 'go' decisions, and once we made that decision, we were only going forward and not back." CIOs know that when you're dealing with so many variables, so many intangibles, a backup plan is nice to have, but in many cases, it's just not possible. Not when you're running against the clock.

So they split the network at midnight on Sunday, September 12, which happened to be Zierhoffer's birthday. If they had problems to deal with, they had six weeks before the official ITT breakup. "We let our fallout happen, and we knew there would be some, and cleaned it up," she said. "It tested our resolve. I allowed no fingerpointing, only teamwork. In the end, when the actual separation date came, it was a nonevent for the IT team."

As with most breakups, you can't separate it all, so an additional important piece was the transition service agreements (TSAs) Zierhoffer's team put in place. "We looked at these as commercially outsourced agreements between the companies, and they needed rigor and teeth," she said. "So we applied the lessons learned of good and bad outsourcing." One of those lessons is that when a company decides to outsource a function, they tend to spend an inordinate amount of time thinking about "getting there" to the outsourced state, but not "living there" in the outsourced state, as she described.

For the transition's sake, she and her team needed to know how to govern it and how to manage it. The TSAs added another dimension. "You have to figure out how to 'get there,' how to 'live there,' and how to *get out of there*,' because you don't want to live in a state where you're buying services from your sister," she said. The relationships weren't very good from a legacy standpoint, never mind once the split occurred and people were in different companies. If you were an accounts payable leader who transitioned to a new company, and you were providing a service to one of the others, you knew where your loyalty was.

Zierhoffer put 23 TSAs in place across ITT. And with them came a critical question: "How long is that TSA going to be in place?" Since they agreed on the time frame, everything would be clear—they knew the cost to provide the services, and they knew the exit plan, cost to exit, and who would pay for each TSA.

Through all the transitions—and all the possible problems and fallout—Zierhoffer maintained her faith in the people around her. "We were a great team, and we were very committed to firefight whatever the hell came our way once we made that decision to go," she said.

But all along the way, there were more pressing people decisions to make. Of all the crucial calls Zierhoffer had to make during the breakup, breaking up her teams might have been the hardest of all.

■ ■ ■

As ITT planned the split, company leaders had decided to name new heads of each function—finance, HR, IT, and so on—for each of the new companies. Once the split happened, the leaders would be in place, ready to go.

For Zierhoffer, though, that philosophy didn't mesh well. She needed her team functioning as one, seeing the whole thing through.

This was yet another key lesson learned from her executive peers: when companies split, things get parochial. Once the switch is flipped, loyalties shift. Human nature would tell anyone moving to a new company that Zierhoffer isn't the boss anymore, and the breakup activities would play second fiddle to the new job—basically the same concern that led her to so strongly insist on and enforce that her role and team was different. They needed to stay together longer. "One team, one mission," she said.

So Zierhoffer went to Loranger and the board and stated her case. Go ahead and name the new heads of finance or HR, she told them, but don't touch IT. She needed her team intact and their loyalties clearly spelled out. Once again, logic prevailed, and Zierhoffer got what she wanted.

Down the road, when the time came to finally slot the IT members into new roles, Zierhoffer found herself fighting once again.

She was speaking with ITT's head of HR after the new-company CIOs had been named. Zierhoffer knew all three and thought that one was far stronger than the others—and would subsequently dominate the others when it came to selecting their teams.

So Zierhoffer told the HR VP that she wanted to sit in on the selection meetings. "You can't," the HR leader told her. "It's not your choice." But Zierhoffer said bad choices would be made, and she could help. Again she heard, "It's not your choice."

It wasn't Zierhoffer's choice, and she knew it. The reason she knew it? That goes back to the very beginning of the story.

When ITT CEO Steve Loranger broke the news, he did say which executives would lead the new companies. And at that time, Loranger told Zierhoffer that he and the board wanted her to become CIO of the aerospace and defense business. It was like someone turned back the clock and put her right smack in the position of when she decided to leave Northrop Grumman.

All of the ITT executives decided to take their roles at the new companies. Except Zierhoffer.

But she did pledge to stay through the breakup. After that, she would go do something else. In her words, she had bigger things to do. Despite driving full-speed through the tumult, the replanning, the bureaucratic headaches, Zierhoffer was never going to enjoy the fruits of her labor. But she stayed through anyway because, well, that's what she said she would do.

And every member of her team that she asked to stay on for breakup did just that. She had won their hearts and minds and gone through a unique experience together.

But it was time to move on. Her next stop would be Xerox, where she served as global CIO until September 2013, when she departed for the Global CIO position at construction giant Bechtel.

■ ■ ■

In the spring of 2013, Zierhoffer spoke before a group of aspiring CIOs at MIT. Her briefing was called "You're the CIO—Now What?"

She's a huge fan of Jim Collins, and she tied two of his popular theories into her presentation. The first was "Greatness is not primarily a function of circumstances; it is first and foremost a function of conscious choice—and discipline." Discipline. That's one of the most important words in her professional vocabulary. And it's one of the most important things she stresses with her teams.

The second: "First who, then what." People come first—always. Leaders have to pick the right people to get on the bus, and they have to make sure they're in the right seats.

Those are Zierhoffer's two foundations, her cornerstones for leadership. And when she finds an imbalance, she doesn't hesitate to make a decisive change.

When she came to Xerox, the company was in the middle of an SAP implementation in Europe, and it wasn't exactly going well. She met with the program manager and his team, and she saw the dysfunction with her own eyes. The manager told her that the PMO's role was to deal with escalations and exceptions only. Zierhoffer responded by asking about the other *E*—her favorite—execution. Who does that? The manager said the subteams actually execute, and he wasn't responsible for that.

She had heard enough. This was not going to work in her mind if, as she said, "the top leader of a multimillion-dollar program doesn't feel accountable for execution, there's a problem." She fired the program manager (he wasn't the right person to be on the bus, and he didn't share her zeal for execution) and put in a call to her old foxhole partner, Steve Little (who was the right person and also had proven his ability to execute).

Zierhoffer also didn't like what she saw in Xerox's information security unit. The group essentially set policy and served as an audit function, but the leader didn't feel he owned the outcomes. Worse, he didn't feel the group had the authority to instruct the company on what needed to be done.

She went to the management committee with a suggestion: Let's bring in an experienced chief information security officer. She wanted a rock-star CISO who would teach the existing leader and the entire organization "what good looked like." It was tough love at work: "You're not the right person for how I envision this role, so I'm going to bring somebody over your head," Zierhoffer told the leader. "But you've got somebody to model after now. Hitch your wagon to this person, and there will be some really great things you can learn."

Zierhoffer had actually done the same exact thing at ITT. In both cases, the person grew under the direction of a more senior leader. Both told her they couldn't believe the difference it made.

Little—who served as interim CIO at Xerox after Zierhoffer's departure—said those examples put her leadership style into clear context. "She's passionate. She's smart as hell," Little said. "She has a way of grasping a situation, understanding it, and dealing with the complex things." Add to that the fact that with so much at stake through the ITT split, Zierhoffer didn't micromanage, Little said.

She actually did one better: "Carol kept the management team in White Plains off our back and let us do our thing," he said. At the end of the day, she said there's no silver bullet for IT, so success comes down to a lot of hard work and execution. And she trusted her team to do just that.

And those are some of the things Zierhoffer brings to her new role as global CIO for Bechtel, the largest construction and engineering firm in the United States and the fifth-biggest privately held company in the land.

■ ■ ■

Zierhoffer also brings another unique tool to Bechtel: She sits on a corporate board of directors.

In April 2013, she was appointed to the board of the MedAssets, which offers financial-management and supply chain–management software to health care organizations. The company was founded in 1998 and went public in 2007; for its 2012 fiscal year, which ended

December 31, the company reported $640.1 million in net revenue, a 10.7 percent jump from the previous year.

And in just a few months, Zierhoffer has made some remarkable strides in accentuating IT's value to the company.

For one, she formed an IT committee on the board, which is something of a rarity at the board level, even with the pervasive influence IT has on corporate operations today. Sharp, successful companies like Walmart, FedEx, and Nationwide have IT committees, and Zierhoffer drew on those examples to form one for MedAssets.

She was recruited to the board to add IT savvy, which the current board members lacked. "Their business and health care expertise is off the charts," Zierhoffer said, "but they recognized a gap." She has a strong partner in John Bardis, the company's founder, chairman, and CEO. He asked Zierhoffer to lead educational sessions about IT at each board meeting—30 to 45 minutes of *each* board meeting. An IT committee is one thing, but devoting that amount of time to IT is practically unheard of.

Overall, her board experience has sharpened her CIO skills. When she was appointed, Zierhoffer reached out to her old boss, ITT CEO Steve Loranger, who gave her a great piece of advice: When you're on a board, it's "nose in, fingers out." In other words, ask great questions, but understand that you're not a part of day-to-day management. "I've been very conscious that it's not my job to run IT; it's my job to ask them very provocative, hard questions that make them think about how they're running IT and help them set strategy," Zierhoffer said. "But it's management's job to actually set the strategy and run the organization."

The last key element she brings to Bechtel is her emphasis on establishing guiding principles—like the Declaration of Independence poster board she used to win buy-in at ITT. When she spoke with the budding CIO group at MIT, Zierhoffer got plenty of questions. The one she heard the most was "Would you send me a copy of those business and IT principles?"

Little said Bechtel is in the best hands possible. And speaking of presentations, he cited another quality Zierhoffer delivers. "It was amazing watching her make a presentation," he said. "She gets people excited. She gives them hope."

CHAPTER 5

The Conductor: Lynden Tennison

Union Pacific is one of the most enduring companies in the history of the United States. The transportation company's origin—commissioned by Congress in 1862 and signed off by President Abraham Lincoln—helped preserve the Union in the throes of the Civil War. From the Missouri River westward, the rail lines offered a new alternative to wagon transportation and contributed greatly to the rise of the American West.

Much has been written about this triumph of construction and expansion. And for years, the company continued to grow. The Staggers Rail Act of 1980 deregulated the industry and nullified restrictions that had been in place since the late 1880s, leading to a new dawn for railroads. Finally, they could run like businesses and focus on growth and profitability.

One of the first things Lynden Tennison will point to is Union Pacific's long legacy of innovation—particularly technological innovation—in the railroad industry. And he'll draw connections between past, present, and future.

As CIO of Union Pacific today, Tennison is paving new ground (almost literally) in innovative new technology and processes that not only save the company money but also—a rarity today—help the company *make* money.

Not long after his appointment as CIO in February 2005, Tennison began tackling the most difficult issue of his tenure.

Union Pacific's transportation management system—think of it like an enterprise resource planning system—which touched practically every critical aspect of the company's business, was written in the 1960s on 11 to 12 million lines of assembler code. As of 2005, very little about that system had changed.

The more than 150-year-old company, with a storied history of innovation, was running an enterprise resource planning system that was almost older than its CIO.

Something had to give.

■ ■ ■

Union Pacific's strengths are in the growth areas of the southern and western United States. As of June 2013, Union Pacific operated in 23 states, covering almost 32,000 route miles. In 2012, the company brought in $3.9 billion in net income and had its most profitable year in its history.

On its website, Union Pacific boasts of having "invested $18 billion in its network and operations to support America's transportation infrastructure, including a record $3.7 billion in 2012," between 2007 and 2012. That 2012 capital investment included installing nearly 4.1 million new railroad ties; replacing 1,050 track miles; purchasing 200 new locomotives; enhancing facilities and building new ones, such as the Santa Teresa, New Mexico, fueling and intermodal facility; and growth and productivity initiatives to improve safety and network capacity.

A considerable chunk—at least in terms of today's "considerable" IT spends—comes from revamping the transportation-management system, the veritable nerve center of the company's vast operations.

When Tennison became CIO, he had already been advocating for a new system. As he saw it, the system wasn't representing the business well—it was outdated, difficult to support and maintain, and difficult to staff.

No one truly owned the system. It was used predominantly by the operations organization but also by marketing, finance, and others. With no defined owner, Tennison saw an opportunity for IT to make a significant strategic contribution to the company. "It was going to be very hard to get anybody but me or the CEO to stand up and say we have to do this, because it's a big, cross-functional technology stack," he said. "This is one of those areas where, to some degree, IT could take a leadership role because [IT] was cross-functional."

Regardless of ownership—or the millions of dollars it would take—Tennison strongly believed it needed to be done. But he'd need to check off a few boxes.

First—although Tennison, like everyone else, doesn't like to admit it—he had to use some political capital. He had a few things going for him on that front. First were his relationships with the core leadership at Union Pacific. Jim Young, who was appointed chairman and CEO shortly before Tennison rose to CIO, and current CEO and President Jack Koraleski were always big believers and advocates in the power of IT. Likewise, several of his peers who headed different functional units saw the huge benefits that would come with an upgraded, more effective transportation-management system.

But relationships aren't everything. Luckily, Tennison and his team had a strong track record to stand on. Working closely with these executives, Tennison's IT shop had delivered many victories for Union Pacific: projects large and small that were successful and impactful. "They knew, in general, that if I made a personal commitment, it would get done," Tennison said. "It was credibility, and it was trust."

This was not to be some overnight decision, though—Tennison didn't make a PowerPoint presentation on Friday expecting board approval on Monday. It took years. Costs, benefits, and risks dominated those lengthy discussions and deliberations.

They knew it would cost many millions, but it was their core, after all. If that system went down, trains stop running, and the business goes in a ditch, as Tennison said.

Drawing on that—plus knowing that the senior management team was willing to take the right risk—Tennison started formulating a plan. The initial estimate for the whole project, dubbed "Net Control," was $200 million over 10 to 12 years.

All the while, he knew the risks. "It was selling it all the way to the board and to the CEO, saying, 'I'm putting my career on the line here,'" said Tennison, who understood all too well the term "betting the farm," being that he grew up working on one. "If this doesn't come through, I'm going to be gone."

■ ■ ■

Lance Fritz, Union Pacific's executive vice president of operations, was serving as a regional vice president at the time the discussions began. He agreed with Tennison's assessment about the new system project.

"It's a bet-the-company kind of proposition," Fritz said. "If [Tennison] either stumbles or gets it wrong, or it doesn't map well to business processes or doesn't give us the flexibility we need over the next three decades, it could be a big issue."

Fritz also pointed to another important aspect of Union Pacific's deliberations over the new system. If the company were a manufacturer, leaders would go out and look for a big ERP system from SAP or Oracle. They'd pick one that fits their processes, and they'd get to work implementing it. "No such tool exists in the marketplace that maps to our business," Fritz said. "Lynden's team is, in essence, rewriting our enterprise system."

When you talk to Tennison about technology tools, he often refers to them as "stuff." He's not demeaning it—it's been his life's career—it's just part of his style.

And when it comes to that stuff, he likes to build it. Tennison is not just a romantic—he is, but the bigger point is that he doesn't want someone else to build it. If you're selling it, there's a good enough chance he's not interested in buying it.

Tennison came to the CIO role packed with experience in leading in-house development teams. Seven years prior to taking the job, he became CEO of a Union Pacific subsidiary called AMCI (later renamed Nexterna), which created private-packet network gear and software for mobile management of locomotives, trucks, and dispatch technicians.

At AMCI, the three partners drew out profits without reinvesting in research and development. Watching that happen provided guidance in how he would later lead various technology subsidiaries as CIO. "One of the things I've insisted over the last eight years in my little technology subsidiaries is that they plow a minimum of 15 percent of revenue back into R&D, because they have to stay current. Otherwise, in technology, you're dead; if you don't stay current, you're dead. You have to continually replow R&D in all aspects of your business. It made it obvious to me that you can't run a really good technology idea for very long as an annuity."

As Fritz pointed out, there was no commercially available solution to the Net Control problem. And Tennison liked to build.

And that's what would happen. Tennison's team would rebuild the transportation-management system.

■ ■ ■

But building internally came with plenty of risks, as his executive colleagues pointed out during their planning discussions.

Right from the start, Tennison began hammering away at some of the major risk profile. While he was confident in the achievements his team had already delivered, Tennison knew he had to prove they could deliver on a much bigger scale.

Step one was to create a proof of concept. Looking at the entire technology stack, Tennison spent $17 million to bring in enough gear to run the workload and mocked a subset to mirror the existing operations. It wasn't the whole thing, mind you—that's why Tennison and his team revved it to 10 times volumes to prove they could scale.

The test was a success. "It validated it to us," Tennison said. "We felt comfortable that we could go up to the chairman and the board and say, 'If we blow up, it's not going to be because the technology can't scale—it's going to be something else.'"

As Tennison began visualizing the way forward after the test, he realized that he couldn't do what many CIOs do when faced with a challenge like this. Instead of pitching a multiyear build that ended with turning the lights on, he gamed out the opposite. Net Control would be incremental build with discreet deliverables along the way.

But that meant building up a new system while running the aging system in parallel. This added risk to an already ambitious aim, but they didn't have much of a choice: they couldn't risk shutting the company down. "You had to say, without a lot of certainty, that we think this is about a $200 million project," Tennison said. "Oh, and by the way, we're going to tear the house down while we're living in it, and build a new one up around it, without stopping the operation."

Driving the project as an incremental build as opposed to a big bang had some notable benefits, though. It was all about continuing to build—and strengthen—credibility with the business. By delivering piece by piece, Tennison said, his team demonstrated that they knew what they were doing, that they could make all the complicated maneuvers, and, most important, that they could deliver benefits all along the way.

But Net Control was still, at its heart, an obsolescence play. And all the test runs in the world couldn't guarantee success—in effect, keeping the railroad company out of that ditch.

■ ■ ■

To get Net Control off and running in the right direction, Tennison called on a few key lessons from his past. One of the most important was his experience—and mastery—of something many CIOs grapple with: truly quantifying success.

Tennison came to Union Pacific after being recruited by Joyce Wrenn, his former boss at American Airlines. Wrenn held senior roles at Bank of America and IBM before coming to American, and she went on from there to hold Tennison's current job at Union Pacific.

While at American, Wrenn ran the advanced technologies group within the Sabre division. (American spun off Sabre into a separate company that went public in 2000.) Wrenn and her direct reports met annually with the division's president to review budget requests for the coming year. As Tennison recalled, they went in with a bunch of "pipe dreams" around the leading-edge technologies with which they dealt, but they expected management would be prepared to cut them down to size. "Everybody knew that was the game going in," he said.

In one particular review, Tennison remembers the other direct reports making their presentations, and it went something like this: *We're doing great things, but we have 100 people, and we need 20 more because of all the projects we still need to deliver.* The president would ask a few questions, and then the finance folks would weigh in and ask more. Predictably, in the eyes of the direct reports, management responded by cutting their existing budgets by 10 percent.

Finally it was Tennison's turn. Outlining his projects from the past year, he went a step further: he calculated that every employee in his organization generated a recurring net return of $285,000 per year, cumulatively, based on revenue. Instead of asking for a big new influx of headcount, Tennison asked for 3. Management told him to add 10.

"It wasn't because I was a superstar," Tennison said. "It was because I had a group that was really good at quantifying the metrics that drove the business." They knew that if they could accurately and definitively measure how their projects drove success, they validated their reason for existence. That's not always easy to do when working on such emerging technologies—"voodoo magic," as Tennison called it—but by capturing those metrics, they could get more resources to drive more results.

That experience would make a huge impact on Union Pacific's current ordeal.

We're talking about a company that runs on metrics, not steam or fuel. They measure everything. Walking into the company's Omaha, Nebraska, headquarters, it's hard to ignore the massive screen highlighting not only warm-and-fuzzy scenic photos but also metrics such as velocity (train speed), weekly carloadings, number of active trains, customer satisfaction, and company stock price. That's what employees see every day, first thing in the morning.

Since Jim Young took over as chairman, Union Pacific has gone from last to first in the industry. There are 12 key metrics the company measures itself against, and in 2012, Union Pacific topped the chart in eight of those categories, including financial returns, operating ratio, net income, and customer satisfaction, which had the biggest margin of victory.

As Tennison and his team trudged through the Net Control project, he knew there would be plenty of meetings that would bring back memories of his budget reviews at Sabre.

Fortunately, he and his team were ready to perform. But that didn't mean everyone was happy about it.

■ ■ ■

About 30 years earlier, at the dawn of the technology era, Union Pacific, like many companies, sent business-savvy clerks and other employees off to learn COBOL. Those were the folks Tennison had keeping the legacy transportation management system humming.

Then came Net Control. All the talk about this new system—along with top executives downplaying the outdated, ineffective legacy system—induced fear and resistance in those ranks.

This group was being thrust into the brave new world of IT—and he was the one thrusting it on them. Highly scalable, horizontal architecture. Web interfaces. Service-oriented architecture. Enterprise service buses. As Tennison explained, they were not exactly thrilled with the prospect of learning all these new technologies.

Initially, the legacy crew feared that they would be fired. It didn't make it any easier when the project began and the longtime Union Pacific employees were working on projects under tech-savvy newer workers, some of whom were studying on college campuses just years before.

Tennison looked at it differently.

Despite all the changes, when you think back, documenting IT initiatives a few decades ago was not quite the process it is today. So in Tennison's eyes, the legacy-system team members weren't relics—they were the institutional memory that, to Union Pacific, was priceless.

"From a functional standpoint, these individuals and their knowledge were crucial. They had the decoder rings. They knew all the deep secrets," Tennison said. "These guys knew all the intimate spaghetti that was in this system. We needed them engaged."

So if he made any clear-throated promises throughout the entire project, one that echoed was his pledge to retain the seasoned legacy team. And he kept his word.

Tennison made another critical move that reinforced his commitment—one that spurred the engagement he needed. Instead of separating the old team and the new, he put them together. There wasn't any sense in doing it differently, he believed. Old or new, they were keeping the trains running. The new system would function the same way as the old one, just with better technology and capabilities. It was all the same to him.

And it brought a nice benefit: by seeing everything that was going on with the old and new systems, Tennison's team members started to find their own niches. For example, those who didn't excel in writing Java code but could design process flows became the business analysts. Careers began to be shaped where many thought there would be no career left at all.

As Union Pacific plowed ahead with Net Control, introducing new module after new module, Tennison stayed firm in not cutting head-count. Sure, a good number of the legacy-system people had reached retirement age, but he wasn't letting his workers go for efficiency's sake.

After all, Net Control wasn't an IT efficiency issue. If it failed, saving jobs could be something of a moot point.

■ ■ ■

That fact wasn't lost on Tennison. Not even a little bit. As he noted, if the Net Control project failed, *he* would be looking for his next job.

Although the project was the most impactful in his career, another situation was more gut-wrenching, and it influenced his perspective on combating the fears of his legacy staff.

When Tennison took the helm at AMCI, the small company was in financial duress, and he had to make some tough decisions. Some of the operating units in AMCI were faltering, and Tennison knew he had to cut them. There he was, realizing that 30 percent or so of the 120 employees would be given their walking papers. "You know it's impacting people and their families," Tennison said. "The cold, callous CEO everyone talks about—I don't know him."

Still, he didn't have a choice. The situation ground at his core. Tennison walked away knowing he had taken the action that was right for the company—but that the events that preceded it were wrong. He was humbled.

That was one eye-opening lesson. Beyond that, he felt that experience gave him the opportunity to look forward—if Tennison would ever find himself in a similar situation, he would be more open and candid with his teams. "People don't need to be perceived as being so mean. You don't want to walk in and everybody thinks life is good, and then you lay 30 people off," he said. "In that sense, we didn't—people knew we were in trouble. But you have to be open. People need to know what's going on as much as possible."

Going forward, Tennison committed himself to openness, to communicating anything and everything. It just so happened that meshed with Young's and Koraleski's philosophy of respect, teamwork, and communication that they expected every Union Pacific executive to live and breathe.

So when he was faced with the quiet rebellion of his legacy team, he knew just how to conduct himself. "You never want to be there again," Tennison said. "You always want to be ahead of that curve."

■ ■ ■

After tackling the fear and uncertainty existing in the legacy team, Tennison also had to watch another potential issue: fatigue.

Every veteran IT professional knows the stress and exhaustion that comes with working on multiyear, multiphase projects. You'll see progress, but after a while, it just feels like running on a treadmill.

So Tennison focused on two remedies. The first was a time-tested management tactic. He rotated people—including his direct reports—in and out of different positions, both inside the IT organization and out. "We gave them some new air to breathe," he said.

The second went to his core strategy for Net Control—and one that many CIOs play very differently. Tennison kept the team focused on the discrete deliverables they mapped for the full project, not on one big-bang initiative. "You have to be able to claim successes along the way—very visible successes," Tennison said in February 2013. "We just did this big cut in our internal systems—hoorah, let's have a big party. If this was a 10-year, flip-the-switch project, this would be a much harder problem."

Most of the projects within Net Control have a 6- to 18-month deliverable, and the results are visible almost instantly. That pace, Tennison said, has made a big impact on reducing the fatigue factor.

And with the piecemeal approach came another opportunity: the ability to quantify the benefits of the project on the fly.

As of July 2013, Union Pacific had spent just under $115 million of the planned $200 million spend for Net Control. And Tennison and his team of 270—which had grown from about 100 at the start—were more than 60 percent done with the project. Of that $115 million, Tennison said about $19 million went to new functionality. That new functionality has already generated $45 million in annual recurring benefits.

At that point, the company was spending somewhere between $20 million and $22 million a year on Net Control, and it was cash-flowing $23 million off the enhancements alone. Union Pacific has also realized an additional $19 million or so in unanticipated enhancements outside the original scope, Tennison said. At the same time, his team had shut down about 58 percent of modules from the legacy system.

Now, Tennison meets with the operating committee—the president and CEO and four executive vice presidents—twice a year to review status, deliverables, upcoming releases, and, of course, risk. Net Control isn't complete, but he sees a pretty bright light at the end of the tunnel.

"We've got about four and a half years left to go, we think, in our current forecast," Tennison said. "Even at the burn rate we're currently at, we're cash-positive. That's a great position to be in."

■ ■ ■

Although Net Control is the big bet that occupies a great deal of Tennison's time, he also holds other responsibilities at Union Pacific that sets him apart from other IT leaders. As CIO, he oversees a number of technology-producing subsidiaries that drive revenue for the company.

Now, Tennison will be the first to tell you that he's not gearing up these organizations to compete with Microsoft in the operating system market or SAP in the broad-based ERP arena. And both he and Fritz said that the total revenue of approximately $25 million is a "rounding error" when it comes to the big picture.

But in the transportation industry, as Tennison said, "We're a big dog." PS Technology, one of those subsidiary companies, provides enterprise workforce management software specializing in rail-crew management and timekeeping tools. Another, Transcentric, offers supply-chain software that gives shippers, carriers, third parties, and trading communities better visibility into inventory, transaction management, and transportation systems support, among key areas.

Tennison's revenue-generating endeavors bring a number of pluses to his organization. It gives his teams some swagger, knowing they can compete in the market. Losses may be humbling, but the experience broadens their horizons. "It builds a different level of expectation and competency within an organization when they know that they're going to have to do this—and that someone else is going to look at it, and they have to want to buy it," Tennison said. "It's no longer a captive audience that has to acquire it."

Owning that technology forces his organization to keep chugging along on the innovation front, as well as working to build better, more sustainable and supportable technology tools.

He's not going to build general ledger or HR systems, but when it comes to transportation-management components, Union Pacific sees plenty of benefit. By having to test their chops in the market, Tennison and his team stay intimately connected to the technology that helps drive their business. "One of the ways to be intimate is to own the product that's the de facto product in the market," he said.

Fritz agreed. "[Tennison's initiatives] keep us engaged with external communities that keep us current on technology and thought," he said. "It also helps us having information flow streams that we wouldn't have otherwise and can benefit from—what someone else is doing, how we can learn from that."

"And, of course, it offsets his cost," Fritz added. "It's beautiful to be able to develop a world-class support product that is subsidized by external sales."

But there are downsides, too. For one, Tennison noted that his teams can't become too enthralled with the idea of commercialization of their efforts. If they do that, next thing you know, they'll be trying to master every database or software system around. "There is a balancing in there," Tennison said. "We need to understand that we are, first and foremost, Union Pacific Railroad's delivery arm."

That also means he can't divert time and energy to a potential $5 million sale that could take away resources from a $100 million deal on the railroad side. The mother ship comes first, Tennison said, and he works vigorously to communicate his subsidiary's objectives with Young, Fritz, and the other C-level leaders at the company. While those executives are supportive of the efforts and express unbending confidence in their CIO, "we are the tail, and they don't want us to wag the dog," Tennison said.

Still, the IT organization's ability to successfully deliver technology to the marketplace surpassed Tennison's expectations when he first took over the CIO role. When he did, his department, which boasted a long tradition of innovation, had, in Tennison's words, become complacent. It's no knock on previous leadership—it was just a sign that it was time to restock and retool the team.

Tennison did that in two ways: aggressively pursuing both experienced hires and college recruiting to get newer, more current skills. Both subsets brought a new level of credibility to the organization, evidenced by a renewed interest from other functional areas of Union Pacific coming to IT to partner.

But as their technological skills improved, those same business partners began challenging the IT organization to bolster its consultative marketing skills. Could his team speak to the business in business terms and translate IT's initiatives into value statements for each function? Could they be a true strategic partner, not just an order taker?

The answer to both—after some hard work—was yes. Tennison and his direct reports took part in customized consulting and marketing workshops, which led them to establish a new marketing plan and branding identity for the organization. His direct reports trained their direct reports, and soon every IT professional at Union Pacific was getting the smarts the business demanded.

And those new competencies have continued to help Tennison and his team sell their technology skills, not only to the outside market but also within Union Pacific, driving massive initiatives like Net Control.

■ ■ ■

Some might look at Tennison's CIO dossier and assume that he had remained true to his developer roots. He drives innovation. He runs technology producers that supply the market. He likes to build stuff internally.

But couple that technical competency with his strong business savvy and emphasis on metrics and performance, and you're looking at the prototype of what many executive search experts, industry thought leaders, and academics point to as the ideal CIO.

"Lynden is not innovating because it's fun and cool, and he's some geeky IT head and it turns him on to be on the cutting edge of IT," Fritz said. "He innovates where it will benefit the core business of Union Pacific and where it will help us differentiate ourselves with our customers in the marketplace. That's an extremely valuable approach and posture to bring to that IT job."

Tennison also acknowledged that his position is different than a solid chunk of CIOs out there. Technology is a core driver of Union Pacific's business, not a necessary evil, as some corporate leaders see it. That's a core contributor to his success: the support of his executive colleagues, all of whom understand the power IT can bring to what many would say is a highly nontechnological industry.

But he has no regrets about being a build-first type of IT leader. Sure, that's unusual in today's business environment, with such a massive number of technology vendors, consulting firms, and systems integrators at CIOs' disposal. "Part of that might be because of the size of our industry and our unique position in that industry. Part of it might be that I, as the CIO, have a bias there, for a number of reasons," Tennison said. "I think it helps us long term with our cost structure. I think it helps us lead from an innovative perspective and to have the bench strength to do what we do. And I'm really not scared of it."

That overall vision permeates his organization. When he meets with his general directors—the group of leaders who sit two rungs below CIO but, in Tennison's words, are the ones who make everything happen—he poses tough questions. In some ways, the tables have turned, and Tennison now sits as the tough interrogators he used to face at Sabre.

He pelts his general directors with a variety of challenges. What areas will grow? Which will shrink? Can we get some efficiencies there?

What are your key risk profiles? Do you have any areas where only one person really knows the job well? If so, we can't have that, so how are you going to fix it? Backfill it? Share it? Build bench strength?

Those are just some of the HR-focused questions. Then comes the really tough one: "If I laid off your entire organization today, who would care?"

Several years ago, his general directors didn't give Tennison the answers he wanted. So he started stressing the importance of metrics, and it took. "That's what's important to our business partners: moving their business metrics," Tennison said. "If you're in the operations department, it's about moving your velocity, moving your crew productivity up, moving your track-gang efficiency up, et cetera. That's what you care about—that's what you're after.

"We were really good at coming in and saying, 'Gosh, we can give you this cool, neat new technology,'" he continued. "But we weren't good at saying, 'Gosh, this cool, neat new technology can drive your metrics.'"

■ ■ ■

When he's not overseeing Net Control, guiding his subsidiaries, or collaborating with his executive peers on what comes next for Union Pacific, Lynden Tennison is probably golfing. Or thinking about golfing.

He's an excellent golfer (well, he says, he "used to be"). He's played in several amateur tournaments, and he currently sponsors a young golfer aspiring to make the professional circuit. Tennison even caddied for the young man during a PGA qualifying tournament.

Tennison clearly enjoys the game—mostly for the mental break he says it provides from work. And he draws some parallels between the two pursuits. For example, golfers and technologists alike need to stay in touch with the latest innovations and tools at their disposal. "You have to stay on your game—you have to continually work at it," Tennison said. "The same thing is true in IT."

He also said he feels like a dinosaur sometimes, leading an IT organization that still builds in-house. So like any good golfer would do when his swing is off, Tennison takes lessons when he wants to stay sharp on the technology side.

A few years ago, he took a Java development class to stay connected and current on his skills. When he came back, one of his best Java developers asked, "So, are you a good developer?"

Tennison replied, in his inimitably humble way, "Even I wouldn't hire me as a Java developer."

CHAPTER 6

The Decider: Wayne Shurts

When *Computerworld* surveyed almost 500 information technology (IT) professionals in August and September 2013, they found an interesting trend developing: More than half of the respondents said they did not aspire to be a CIO.

That probably didn't shock too many sitting CIOs. After all, only those leaders truly know the monumental tasks, pressures, and constant change that they're forced to endure, day in and day out. And truth be told, at one point in their career, many CIOs—including some of the best in the business—did not exactly have their sights set on the perch.

Take Wayne Shurts. Early in his career, at Nabisco, Shurts gained leadership experience in finance, sales, and marketing. Back then, moving into the IT domain wasn't on his radar. But when he was tapped to lead a sales transformation project at Nabisco, IT became a major part of his portfolio.

Back then, Nabisco had an industry-leading direct store delivery model. The truck driver would unpack the goods at a grocery store, and the sales representative would both stock the shelves and displays and sell to the store manager. The first non-Nabisco employee to touch a Nabisco product was the consumer, and the process was powerful. The problem was that it was costly.

Nabisco knew that 80 to 90 percent of the sales representatives' work involved physical labor, stocking the shelves. That meant they were spending too little time talking with the store managers, selling incremental product displays, and other value-added sales activities.

And this was at a time when Nabisco was first starting to harness the power of data. What they knew at the time was that they had roughly a 40 percent market share, and top competitor Keebler registered at about 25 percent. But if you looked at the store shelves, the two companies' products had equal space. Nabisco wanted their sales representatives to work to demonstrate Nabisco's advantage. The more shelf space it had, the more products Nabisco could sell.

Nabisco's executive leadership brought in McKinsey to consult and put Shurts in charge of redesigning the sales force. So Shurts pulled together a project team, including some young stars from the field sales force, and they developed a plan. In addition to upgrading systems, processes, and technology—including a new ordering tool that would harness the data they had on each store—they needed more bodies at a cheaper cost. So they would increase territory size (in other words, fewer sales reps) and supplement with lower-paid merchandisers who could do the physical work, giving sales representatives more capacity to sell. The teams would become more efficient, and the company would have lower costs, the thinking went.

They targeted three or four markets to run a pilot in an eight-month time frame. After making any necessary tweaks, the national rollout would take between 18 and 24 months, according to Shurts. But the Nabisco leadership wanted results more quickly.

Their only option: cut out the eight-month piloting period. The result: As Shurts described it, "It was an unmitigated disaster."

Fast-forward almost two decades later. Shurts has built a strong career and reputation as a CIO, first at Cadbury, then Supervalu, before becoming chief technology officer at Sysco. Longtime colleagues like Tom Garvin, an executive consultant to the Business Technology group at Sysco, cite a number of key leadership principles that propelled Shurts to success.

Still, Shurts is the first to point out that, while those principles were strengthened through his leadership journey, they were forged by failure.

■ ■ ■

Reflecting on the sales transformation project at Nabisco, which took place in the mid-1990s, Shurts acknowledges that they rolled it out too fast. They hadn't perfected the overall model. They brought in merchandisers, but they didn't do the right level of knowledge transfer with them. At certain points, store shelves were bare of Nabisco products. The plan was to improve the sales process, but the failed planning and rollout did the opposite.

"It was not good," Shurts said. "It was probably the first failure—a really big failure—that I ever had, and it really stung."

Important lessons came to the forefront immediately. That was a positive development, and a necessary one, because Shurts was about to get a shot at redemption.

Right after the sales project went south, Shurts began taking stock of what went wrong. And that was one of the first and most important lessons he learned. Instead of focusing on what's right in your plan, Shurts said, you have to be "relentless" in determining what's wrong, and what might not work. Things will go wrong on any project—the key is to pay close attention to detail and understand that the plan you put on paper will likely be different than what's really going to work in the field.

Another key lesson centered on time. Some things cannot be rushed; sometimes you need to take the extra time to do it right. Had they had their eight-month testing window, Shurts and his team probably would have spotted flaws and been able to course-correct on the spot. Shurts now chides himself for letting this important task be hurried into failure.

And just as he was licking his wounds, a new opportunity emerged. Nabisco was running on AS400 at the time, and the sales representatives and merchandisers were using "dumb" handheld terminals in the stores. They had the data on each store, but sales representatives didn't have the right tools to maximize their up-selling opportunities. If they went to a grocery store, the only way the sales team knew what level to order at was by memory.

That ordering tool Shurts had wanted to implement before was now an absolute necessity. Nabisco wanted to bring in SAP to replace the legacy system, and its leaders wanted Shurts to lead the project.

So Shurts quit sulking and got to work. But he promised himself something: "I was never going to forget how crappy that last assignment felt, how hard those lessons were learned," he said. "I was never going to let that happen again."

■ ■ ■

The mission, as Shurts saw it, wasn't about putting in SAP—it was about eliminating situations where Nabisco products were out of stock in the stores. After crunching the numbers, Nabisco had found that the out-of-stock issue was much bigger than previously thought.

They had sales representatives in the stores taking orders each week, so how could they have a problem? It turned out that 8 percent of items were out of stock at any given time, and a lot of those times were weekends, when grocery stores saw their highest shopping traffic.

So, they asked, why? It must be because the closest warehouse didn't have those products in stock. But that was true only one-third of the time. For the remainder, it was because the sales representatives hadn't reordered the product in their last order for the item that was out of stock.

All in all, Shurts said, correcting the errors—and giving the sales team a better suggested order volume for new stores—represented a $50 million profit opportunity for Nabisco.

But it wasn't a simple rip-and-replace situation. To do it right, he would need the time he hadn't had for the last project.

Another key lesson he learned from the sales-transformation project was the importance of working with the people in the field—and actually being out in the field. Shurts will tell you that the best systems are designed on the warehouse floor, in the stores, in the restaurants—wherever the work gets done, with the people who do the work. You can only do so much from headquarters.

"We were incredibly engaged with the field in terms of what was working and what wasn't," Shurts said. "We designed it with the field, not just in headquarters, and we went out there to pilot it and test it."

Shurts and his team went to the Edison, New Jersey, sales branch to begin the pilot. They realized right away that they couldn't run both the AS400 systems and the new SAP system in parallel. So for six weeks, they sent a large team to Edison after normal business hours to develop the SAP side in the sandbox. They duplicated everything that happened during the day on the AS400 system on the SAP system—every order, every invoice, and so on.

During the testing, the systems integrator was telling Shurts that he was ready to go. Shurts said no—they were testing for a reason, and there would be no shortcuts. And during those six weeks, they found a number of issues that, as Shurts recalled, "would have screwed us up big-time." Two or three weeks after the testing, they had corrected the issues.

Then they went live in Edison, and they kept the new system isolated there for another three months. All the while, they worked out any remaining kinks in the software—Shurts said they had three new versions in that time—and then got to work rolling it out to the other 130 sales branches across the United States.

The sales representatives got new pen-pad computers that generated suggested orders for new stores. The application made them walk through the shelves from left to right, methodically, to check inventory. If they weren't going to order a product, they actually had to enter a zero. In other words, the software helped keep them accountable—and they could more quickly spot any potential out-of-stock problems.

The project was a success. In the late 1990s, Nabisco had the biggest transactional system on SAP in North America, with approximately 13,000 invoices generated a day and a dramatic reduction in store-level out-of-stocks.

■ ■ ■

As Shurts explained, that shot at redemption became the experience that catapulted him into the CIO stratosphere. He made one more stop, though, before he claimed the role.

While he was successfully implementing the SAP system at Nabisco, Shurts was reading headline after headline about enterprise resource planning (ERP) failures. Many IT professionals remember when massive systems problems kept Hershey Foods from delivering $100 million worth of candy for the 1999 Halloween season. And the stories have gone on and on.

Shurts recruited Tom Garvin and two other partners to form Principles Group, a consulting firm that would help companies tackle difficult ERP implementations. They knew the technology worked, he said, and that most of the problems companies faced were organizational, not technical, so Principles Group would be the change management agent.

The firm launched on September 1, 2001, with obviously no knowledge of how the world would so dramatically change 10 days later. Still, through the challenging economy that followed, the team charged ahead. Shurts learned some invaluable lessons as a business owner, but he also got some reminders about the power of working at a large corporation that could fund necessary initiatives.

Then he got a call from Jim Chambers, a former mentor and Nabisco executive who was then CEO of Cadbury's Americas business. Chambers was looking for someone to run IT in the Americas; Shurts was loving the consulting world, and he had no desire to leave.

But because he had great respect for and a longstanding relationship with Chambers, he listened. And the more he listened, the more intriguing the possibility became. And the more intriguing it became, the more it dawned on Shurts that while he had stood in the shoes of the executives he was consulting with, the world was changing so fast that if he didn't get back in those shoes at some point, he'd become something of a dinosaur.

He accepted the job in early 2006 and was named senior vice president of IT. (Principles Group still exists today, with Shurts's brother Doug, a former AT&T executive, at the helm along with one of the original partners.) And two short years later, he was offered the global CIO role. Once again, he needed some convincing. Shurts ended up speaking with a senior finance executive at Cadbury, who posed an interesting question. "He said to me, 'I don't understand how you want to be in IT but you don't aspire to be the CIO,'" Shurts recalled. "It kind of hit me, and it stuck with me. With the encouragement of several trusted peers, I looked at it and said, 'Things at Cadbury need to be transformed. If not me, then who?' And instead of resisting, I leaned in wholeheartedly."

In one fell swoop, Shurts went from not being sure if he wanted the job to wanting it in the worst way. He felt he had the right tools and ideas to help the company.

And that shines a light on a career perspective that, among most elite IT leaders, is the exception, not the rule. Shurts has taken on different roles at different companies, and while he jokes that his resume looks a bit "schizophrenic," it's more an illustration of what drives his decision making. At the core of that is a simple question he asks himself: Where can I add the most value? Earlier in his career, he had never imagined the answer would be as a CIO.

"Each move was going to the next place where I thought I could add the most value and make the most improvement," he said. "So it's always where can I add value, not necessarily where can I climb the ladder."

There were plenty of reasons to say no. The job wouldn't be easy—there were a number of fires to put out, and he'd be doing it while traveling extensively, spending more time on the road than with his family. But when he focused his internal deliberation on that simple question, he had his answer.

■ ■ ■

At first, Shurts hadn't known if he wanted to leave consulting; then he wasn't sure about taking on the global role. But once he got into that role, one thing was for sure: he was loving every minute of it. Working in emerging markets excited him, as did the amount of agile IT innovation taking place, despite limited budgets.

But in January 2010, after extensive negotiations that began after a hostile takeover bid, Kraft acquired Cadbury for just under $19 billion.

Shurts spent the first quarter of the year flying to Chicago to work on the acquisition with Kraft's then CIO. At the same time, knowing the writing was on the wall, he started looking for his next move. A number of opportunities popped up, but one stood out: Supervalu, the Eden Prairie, Minnesota–based grocery store giant.

Shurts had always been on the manufacturing side of the food business, and the retail side was alluring, mainly because of the sheer volume of data those companies owned, analyzed, and controlled.

But Supervalu was also in turnaround. Four years earlier, it had acquired Albertsons for $9.7 billion. (CVS and Cerberus Capital Management also bought pieces of the company.) At the end of its 2009 fiscal year, though, Supervalu had reported a net loss of $2.86 billion from revenues of $44.6 billion.

Shurts said he might have been "a glutton for punishment," but he wanted that turnaround experience.

Early in the interview process, Shurts started learning more about one of the turnaround's main culprits. When the company bought Albertsons, it acquired a number of grocery-store chains it owned, including Shaw's, Acme, and Jewel. Albertsons had acquired those companies when it bought American Stores in 1998.

But there was a big problem: American Stores had never integrated the systems of its operating companies (or "banners"), and each banner had its own merchandising organizations. Supervalu's solution was an initiative called "Superfusion," which aimed to centralize the sprawling merchandising and retail functions and take advantage of the potential combined buying power of what was then a $36 billion retail company.

By the time Shurts arrived as CIO in April 2010, Supervalu was three years into Superfusion, and the price tag to that point was about $200 million. And the company was way behind schedule. Supervalu had begun implementing a common retail and merchandising system, but the company still had a jumble of systems under the hood. They just couldn't seem to get Superfusion straight. Part of that was because the original champions of the program—the chief merchandising officer and the CIO at launch time—had both left Supervalu a year and a half into Superfusion.

It was so bad, Shurts said, that the team had kept asking for more time and more money. One year before he arrived, they went to the board, saying it would take an extra year beyond what was planned, and it would cost another $50 million. Six months later, they did the same thing. When Shurts arrived, another six months was up, and the board was hearing the same cry for help.

People were telling Shurts that with those extensions and additional funding infusion, they'd be fine. But the new CIO was looking at the company's state, and from his perspective anything that was going to take three years wasn't very helpful in turning Supervalu around.

Superfusion had devolved into just an IT project—not a business transformation initiative. There were chronic delays with no end in sight. Few thought it would work.

Business leaders were asking Shurts if he could rectify Superfusion in enough time to help the company's turnaround. Even if the planned extensions worked, it would be too late, and it would cost money Supervalu couldn't afford to spend.

In his second week as CIO, Shurts went around the room, asking the company's senior leaders why they were still doing Superfusion. No one could give him a credible answer.

In his sixth week, he pulled the plug.

■ ■ ■

Shurts quickly developed a new strategy: To accept the fact that the disparate systems were the reality, and instead of continuing a long, costly, unproductive ERP implementation, fast, agile guerrilla tactics would rule the day. "They were probably the antithesis of one another," Shurts said.

The IT organization would shift its focus to creating "business transformation" tools—applications that would go on top of the existing systems, but would allow store directors to make better decisions on inventory, shrink, promotions, and other key objectives. The executive team stood behind him, thankful that someone finally made the call. The IT team was heavily invested in the project, but most agreed that Shurts's strategy was the right move.

Most.

One sticking point was how Shurts described the kind of applications they needed to create. *Good enough* was the term he used repeatedly. Some on the IT team didn't appreciate that—they had been striving for perfection, and the more Shurts examined the past delays, he found that that attitude was one of the primary causes of those delays.

The way those IT pros saw it, "good enough" meant "sloppy." They thought that Shurts's approach would lead to new applications with defects. If it wasn't perfect, they seemed to be saying, it was just plain wrong.

"Rather than designing for the rule and accommodating the exception, they were designing everything to be perfect, perfect, perfect," he said. "So we came out and said, 'Something better today—especially at Supervalu—was worth far more than something perfect a year from now.'"

And he continued to stress the business context. The platform was burning, he told them, though he got the feeling that many didn't realize it. Months later, they still had people in pockets of the IT organization who were holding on to the past. Shurts likened them to Japanese soldiers in World War II on isolated islands who, despite their nation's surrender, kept fighting anyone they could find (some, reportedly, almost 30 years later).

Shurts was able to combat that posturing by showing results: a few successes here and there started building momentum, and once they had it, the IT workers began to believe in the strategy. It also helped that they found the new mission more fun than their previous toiling over the ERP implementation.

"It took a whole behavioral change and change in thinking, from delivering great benefits to this company later, and later, and later, to delivering value today," Tom Garvin said. "It's a principle Wayne carries with him and through the organization: You have to work with what's real. Otherwise, what are you doing? You're pretending."

Shurts cooked in a few more important tactics as well. He created a business-immersion program, which mandated that every IT employee had to spend a few days in the field. For instance, if employees supported warehouse management systems, they would spend a few days actually working in a warehouse, utilizing the system. The idea behind it was that getting that exposure in the field would energize them to improve their systems when they returned. And it worked.

In addition, Shurts felt the IT organization had too much bureaucracy, undeniably a relic of the ERP project. If they were going to be fast and agile, they couldn't be hampered by all the existing sign-off and project management policies. So he created a task force he called "IT Simplified." He brought together a team to investigate their core processes and find new, faster methods. The process owners didn't initially like the results, but Shurts and his leadership team got them on board, in part by using the same argument they had used to reel in the timid, perfection-demanding technologists.

But still, too many of the technical people wanted an exact game plan for handling every imaginable situation; if they were given a task, they wanted to be told to do X. Shurts pushed back, positing that if they tried to create a road map for every possible scenario, they'd end up muddled in bureaucracy once again.

To break the impasse, Shurts and his team introduced a new phrase to the organization: "Think and Respond." It started with the principle that they needed to be fast, delivering "good enough" solutions in three weeks or three months, not three years, and included technical problem-solving principles. "That's all the picture you need," Shurts told them. "You are smart, intelligent professionals whom I hired for your brains, not for you to be a monkey who follows some preconceived, day-in-the-life process."

The message was clear: Take action. Forget about the bureaucratic days of the past, when IT workers on the front lines had to wait for decisions from three layers above—those days were long gone. Think about each situation, and then respond by doing the right thing. As Shurts saw it, if employees thought about and responded to 20 percent of their objectives in the wrong way, that was fine, because that meant that the other 80 percent would have been right.

Tom Garvin, who served as a consultant to the IT leadership team at Supervalu, described the credo as "liberating" for the organization.

Shurts had come into his new role and, in what seemed like the blink of an eye, put a stop to a bulky, misguided, money-gouging ERP project. He created a new strategy on the fly. In the process, he reshaped the entire culture of the organization. And he got results: The new applications rolled out to store directors, and the company saw notable improvements in key areas like inventory and ordering efficiency.

■ ■ ■

In the different offices he has occupied over the years, there's one mainstay for Shurts: a photo of Abraham Lincoln visiting General George McClellan and his troops at Antietam in October 1862, less than a month after their bloody victory over the Confederate Army. If you look closely at the president's pant leg, there appears to be mud all over it. "Even Abraham Lincoln, the president during the Civil War, was getting dirty," Shurts said.

For Shurts, it goes back to that failed project at Nabisco. A big part of that is getting out in the field. And a byproduct of that is understanding exactly whom he and his team serve.

In an October 2013 town hall, Shurts emphasized to his team at Sysco the importance of caring—both about their operating companies and about their customers. One way to demonstrate that, he said, is by getting out there. Shurts takes issue with people and companies that don't believe that "corporate" works for its customers and employees, and not the other way around. "It's amazing how many companies have that backwards," he said. "They think the people in the field work for corporate, and that's a bad habit we need to break."

Shurts also sees a disconnect in many IT organizations. Too often, he said, IT professionals hide behind ticket systems. We all know how it goes: An employee reports an IT problem, and a ticket is generated. The ticket then goes to a level 1 help desk, and sometimes up to level 2, until the problem is resolved—a rigid, basically robotic process.

But as Shurts tells his teams, on the other end of that ticket is a real, live person or customer with what could be a serious problem. They might not be able to bill a customer because of a glitch, or maybe they can't deliver food to a store because of a system outage. And in a lot of cases, that real, live person or customer is going to be upset. And for his team, it's important to understand why. "You've got to get your nose rubbed in the dirty reality of the business to stay grounded in what you're really trying to accomplish," Shurts said, "and not sit safely and comfortably behind these ticket processes we like."

He thinks back to the old TV show, Mutual of Omaha's *Wild Kingdom*. The host, Marlin Perkins, had a sidekick, Jim Fowler, who always did the dirty work. Shurts recalled Perkins sitting safely in his boat while describing how Jim was busy wrestling a wild alligator. He wants his people to be like Jim, wrestling the wild alligators. And he'd rather be Abraham Lincoln, getting dirty alongside his troops.

■ ■ ■

There's another thing about that Lincoln photo that Shurts doesn't point to, but it applies to his leadership—and how he motivates his teams. When Lincoln visited McClellan that day at Antietam, historians have recounted, he was actually encouraging the general to go back after the Confederates, as the September 1862 victory was not decisive enough to truly turn the tide in the Civil War.

Go fight the competition. That's what Shurts, as a CIO, has encouraged his teams to do, a century and a half later.

Along with that, the lessons from his first failure—focusing on what could go wrong, taking the time to do things right, and anticipating roadblocks—apply as well. "Those lessons are ingrained in my *soul*," Shurts said. "When you start managing these major projects at the sound-bite level, you get in trouble."

And that takes him back to another key lesson he's learned through his career: You have to take care of the basics of IT before you can earn the right to have the bigger, more strategic conversation. "My platform for pushing this new vision is only as good as the core services that I'm delivering to the business—and they drastically need improvement," Shurts said. "If I started making this the main item on my agenda, my business partners would come back at me and say, 'Why don't you go back and fix your shop so we can get the basic business right? Then we can talk about the bigger vision.'"

That's just fine with Shurts. Making tough decisions is a hallmark of his career, and there will undoubtedly be more of those choices to make—though that's not how he sees it. "It's odd how many times I've come in and just done the obvious, right thing that no one else did, and you hear that it was such a 'hard, brave decision,'" he said. "I'm no genius here—it was just obvious."

That demonstrates a key character trait that Tom Garvin points to that separates Shurts from most business leaders: humility. Whether participating in an executive meeting, speaking to the board of directors, sitting with his leadership team, speaking at a town hall or buying coffee at the local Starbucks, Garvin said Wayne carries himself the same way, speaking eye to eye—not speaking down from his C-level position. "Primarily Wayne cares about people. It's people we lead—not projects and programs," Garvin said, echoing Shurts's position. "And we are all people."

Away from work, Shurts treasures time spent with his family and rooting for his New York Giants (he's a season ticket holder), New York Yankees, New Jersey Devils, and all the teams from his alma mater, Lehigh University. But when it comes to work, his real passion is solving problems and adding value. And knowing that his IT organizations can make his employees' and customers' lives easier makes all the difference.

"Therein lies the magic, and where the world is going," Shurts said. "And it's actually a lot of fun."

CHAPTER 7

The Realist: Don Imholz

n the fall of 2007, Don Imholz made a big decision: after more than 30 years in the defense and aerospace business with McDonnell Douglas and Boeing, he was ready to try something new.

Consulting opportunities abound, and after decades of constant travel, Imholz looked forward to more time at home with his wife and family. He still traveled, though, and one night in early 2008, after flying to California to visit a client, he got a curious voice mail.

Carol Goldman, the chief administrative officer at Centene, asked him to call back. Centene, a health care services company, launched in 1984 in St. Louis, where Imholz spent his entire professional career. But he'd hardly heard of it.

When he called back, Goldman cut to the chase: Would he be interested in interviewing to become the company's new CIO? The company was growing rapidly, facing new and exciting challenges. Imholz was easing into retirement, staring at speaking and advisory gigs. Still, he agreed to meet with her.

Centene was looking for an experienced IT executive to join its leadership ranks. The company had seen an almost 25 percent increase in revenue in 2007 over the previous year, and they knew there was more to come. When company executives and board members asked around for recommendations, they kept hearing the name Don Imholz.

But he said he wasn't ready to go back to work. He'd consult, though, Imholz told them.

A few months went by, and Imholz got another call. It was Centene's CFO, asking Imholz if he had changed his mind. No, Imholz said, but he'd be happy to consult.

A few more months later, a local consulting-firm owner, Joe Blomker, got a call from the CFO. Centene was desperate for an IT leader. Did he know anyone? Sure, Blomker said—he had a guy who could help on a consulting basis. "What's his name?" the CFO asked. "Don Imholz."

It was no coincidence. St. Louis might be a large city, but small worlds exist everywhere. Imholz and Blomker were close friends, and they had a handshake agreement to bring each other into projects that met the other's specialties—for Imholz, strategic projects; for Blomker, more technical implementations.

The three men met across the street from Centene's corporate headquarters. At that point, the CFO gave in to Imholz's insistence on consulting. "If I can't get you full time, I'll take what I can get," Imholz recalled the CFO telling him.

And so it began. Imholz put together a short-term advisory proposal and an assessment of Centene's current IT operation. Before he knew it, he was invited to interview prospective CIO candidates—just a part of long weeks at the company.

And before he knew it, he was being roped in. By the middle of August 2008, Imholz had gone from "no way" to a full-time role, to "maybe." He went home and told his wife that Centene wanted him to work full-time. She said, "I thought you already were working full time. . . ." In early September 2008, Centene announced Imholz as its new CIO.

Moving from the defense and aerospace business to health care is not a jump many IT leaders make—or could even handle. Moreover, the thought of changing industries is a massive leap—again, one that some can't handle. But Imholz is a unique CIO.

Reflecting on that transition in a June 2013 interview, Imholz pointed to the skill sets he had grown to make that shift possible. He grew those through one of the most challenging times of his career, when he found himself at the forefront of a cataclysmic development that would reshape the IT industry as the world knew it.

■ ■ ■

Through more than 30 years in the business world, Don Imholz witnessed some of the most earth-shattering changes to the way companies deploy technology.

Mainframes, client-server technology, digitization, mobility— you name it. Every few years, another big change to the landscape.

But there was one game-changer to IT for which Imholz had a front-row seat: IT outsourcing.

In 1989, Eastman Kodak opted to farm out its IT operations. The company sold its mainframe computers to IBM, which would then run its IT. The 10-year, $3 billion deal not only established IBM as an IT services provider but also effectively introduced the term *outsourcing* (as a business strategy, at least) into the corporate lexicon.

Kathy Hudson, director of information systems at Kodak, clearly explained the logic behind the decision in a *Fortune* magazine article in September 1991. "IBM is in the data-processing business," Hudson said, "and Kodak isn't."

For Imholz, who steadily rose up the corporate ranks at aerospace giant McDonnell Douglas, the shift toward outsourcing wasn't necessarily new, and in many cases, it made perfect business sense. When he started his career there, McDonnell Douglas directly employed all the cafeteria workers, janitors, and groundskeepers who worked at the company headquarters in St. Louis.

"Over time, when you're paying aerospace wages and you have a common benefit package, those get to be a pretty expensive approach," Imholz said. "More importantly, you're just not good at those things—you don't pay attention to those things.

"They're commodities to buy, and they're not easy to undo," he continued. "So those things go."

Not long after the Kodak deal, McDonnell Douglas fell on hard times. The company's defense business faced a changing industry with more and more competition. McDonnell Douglas faced a liquidity crisis, and the CFO had to take a hard look at the multitude of assets the company had stockpiled.

What was strategic, and what was not? That was the big question. Today, companies have a lot to work with when making an outsourcing decision—more than two decades worth of case studies; seasoned, specialized consultants and advisors; all the best-practices lists you could imagine. McDonnell Douglas had what they could glean from Kodak, but that was about it.

This, almost literally, had never been done before.

One of the nonstrategic assets identified was the in-house computing services division. Outsourcing it, the CFO surmised, could be a viable way to bring in cash and focus the company on its core competencies. The thinking was not very different from Kodak's, which faced similar strategic decisions.

And like Kodak, McDonnell Douglas began negotiations with IBM. Imholz, who was serving as general manager of the computing services division at the time, didn't necessarily agree that outsourcing was the right move. But the writing was on the wall.

Imholz knew he could be facing all the classic challenges that come with major outsourcing—potential drops in performance, cultural shifts, employees worrying about their careers.

And once the deal was done, he wondered, where would he land?

■ ■ ■

Ask most IT leaders about their history of IT purchasing decisions, and they'll probably highlight their successes while maybe—maybe—briefly mentioning those that didn't go so well. Ask Don Imholz, and you'll get the full story.

For example, he's not afraid to talk about his decisions around word processing. As a rising IT leader at McDonnell Douglas during the dawn of the PC era, Imholz was charged with finding a product that could help the company reduce clutter and take advantage of computing power.

He looked at *PC* magazine and saw IBM's Displaywriter product moving up the best-seller charts. But 18 months later, they decided to go in a different direction. The choice this time was between WordPerfect, the popular, well-established tool from Corel, or a newcomer to the market called Microsoft Word.

The company was just about split. The slight majority wanted WordPerfect, primarily for functionality reasons. The slight minority picked Word.

WordPerfect won. "I was in the middle of that decision," Imholz said, "so I went 0 for 2."

But he's had more than his fair share of wins. Take the time Imholz led the project to revamp McDonnell Douglas's human resources system. He heard about a young start-up in Silicon Valley that had maybe a few dozen customers but was far from the market leader.

Imholz and McDonnell Douglas's HR chief flew out to Walnut Creek, California, to spend some time with the team and its founder, Dave Duffield. Duffield convinced them that his company, PeopleSoft, would make it. McDonnell Douglas bought the HR application, and years later, it became one of the first customers for PeopleSoft's finance platform. About 20 years later, they're both still in production. "Good for them; good for us," Imholz said. (Duffield sold PeopleSoft to Oracle in 2004 for $10.3 billion and went on to found Workday, which, as of November 15, 2013, had a market capitalization of $13.14 billion.)

When CIOs choose right, many other business leaders just think it was easy. When they choose wrong, most point at the CIO and ask, "What were you thinking?" Regardless, Imholz paints choices like these—big software purchases or outsourcing decisions—as the toughest for IT leaders to make. They take time. They're expensive. And they disrupt the business.

In his career, Imholz has been involved in several bet-the-farm decisions. Working through the McDonnell Douglas outsourcing question would be the toughest of all.

■ ■ ■

Following the Kodak outsourcing deal, many industry experts expected every major corporation would start farming out their IT operation. It didn't take off like wildfire, but several big deals followed in the succeeding years.

At the end of fiscal year 1992, McDonnell Douglas, then the largest weapons contractor in the United States, reported an earnings decrease of about 62 percent. Its C-17 cargo plane line was bleeding money, as was its commercial aircraft division.

IBM came knocking. McDonnell Douglas was sitting on large real estate holdings and a healthy helping of mainframe computers. IBM offered to buy the buildings and buy the computers—and take all the in-house support team members Imholz oversaw.

Again, the CFO, Herb Lanese, immediately saw an opportunity. "His view was 'Hey, it's just computers,'" Imholz recalled about the finance chief. "His view—right or wrong—was 'IBM knows how to manage computers. Why wouldn't we go with IBM, or EDS?'"

IBM was ready to pay, and IBM could manage the technology better. But not everyone agreed.

Technology was changing rapidly at the time. Mainframes were giving way to distributed computing, among other innovations. And with that, Imholz said, many business leaders saw IT as the company's lifeblood. McDonnell Douglas, the thinking went, was an engineering company that manufactured sophisticated products. If it didn't have the most up-to-date computer systems, how could it design the next generation of aircraft?

At the end of the day, though, differences of opinion mattered little. The computing services organization reported up to the CFO, and the company needed money. When a company falls into financial distress, the CFO can have an inordinate amount of decision-making authority.

Imholz knew he had to put his own reservations aside. He had no idea where he would end up, but for the good of the company, he soldiered on.

He tried to be as transparent as possible with his 1,400 employees. Even before McDonnell Douglas signed the 10-year, $3 billion outsourcing agreement with IBM, Imholz communicated what was under way. He told them that the winning bidder was considering hiring the entire team.

To Imholz, the idea of working at IBM wasn't the worst. "If you're an IT professional, you can make the argument that it's good to work for an IT company rather than an aerospace company," he said.

But he was talking about his employees. Imholz would have to make his own decisions.

■ ■ ■

All 1,400 employees did get job offers from IBM. Some declined, but most took the opportunity.

Imholz knows several who stayed and actually retired from IBM. For those who wanted to thrive in IT, IBM, as Imholz predicted, became a great breeding ground.

He also knows people who flamed out quickly. There was a down-side to the IBM opportunity for some—if they knew aerospace and wanted a career in the industry, moving into the technology sector wasn't the best match.

Imholz faced the same dilemma. Just before the deal closed, he didn't know his own future. The good news was that Imholz wasn't very worried. Prior to his role overseeing the computing-services division, he held senior IT leadership roles in McDonnell Douglas's aircraft division and had relationships and respect over there.

Still, if McDonnell Douglas didn't offer him a good opportunity, IBM would be happy to. "IBM made that known to us subtly," Imholz said, "but in some cases, not so subtly."

But Imholz had decided to make a career in aerospace. He'd spent 18 years learning all about the highly complex industry, and he wasn't going to let that be for naught.

About two weeks before McDonnell Douglas completed the deal with IBM, Imholz became head of IT for the company's aircraft business. Of all the opportunities he thought he'd have, Imholz didn't see that one coming. And in an interesting twist, he instantly became IBM's biggest customer.

A few years later, Imholz moved out of IT and into the business side of the aircraft division. He had made a few forays into the business before, but this opportunity would be more lasting. Imholz rotated into various finance positions, part of a succession management plan. He had an undergraduate degree in business, a master's degree in information technology, and was sponsored by the company to get his executive MBA. His finance rotations allowed him to match his business experience with his education.

In August 1997, McDonnell Douglas merged with rival Boeing in a $13 billion stock swap. Through the transition, Imholz was plucked from finance and appointed CIO of the combined company's defense business. Several years later, Boeing consolidated all IT operations, and Imholz was appointed to lead most of the companywide application development and support organization, in addition to being CIO of the defense business. Later, he was responsible for all application development and support.

These were great years for Boeing, with record orders. Having been in a cyclical business for his entire career, Imholz knew the good times would not last forever, so it was a good time to try something new.

■ ■ ■

It's tough to say if the IBM outsourcing deal saved McDonnell Douglas. It undoubtedly boosted liquidity, which was a major issue at the time. But there were other initiatives under way to revive the company.

In that industry, cash comes in big chunks. One executive told Imholz that McDonnell Douglas sold a few more MD-11 aircraft than expected, which led to a big cash infusion.

Still, the deal made a lot of sense, despite some of the internal turmoil it caused. "It was cash- and expense-driven," said Ken Lawler, a senior finance leader at McDonnell Douglas during that time. "But people also don't realize that IBM had these big centers, and they had multiple clients that would share the expense. So they could generate economics in that environment."

Either way, it taught Imholz a lot about making decisions in the best interest of the company. Today, when looking at outsourcing opportunities, Imholz looks at core versus context. Companies do better when they know where they want to excel and what will help their brand, market presence, and competitiveness.

He thought back to all the cafeteria workers, janitors, and grounds-keepers McDonnell Douglas once employed. Overall, corporate America has shifted dramatically in that direction—but Imholz said it's more complicated when it comes to IT.

Sometimes there are clear-cut decisions. He gave the example of database management. Thirty years ago, companies ran their own systems; today, with ubiquitous vendor offerings, not many would go with the in-house option.

But companies decide to outsource functions like helpdesk or application development for a variety of reasons: It could be pure cost efficiencies, for performance improvement, or for a number of other justifiable priorities. "The right way to do it is first, strategy, then financial analysis, and then pick your partner. If you do that, I think things will work fine," Imholz said. "I'm not all-in one way or the other—I'm not all-in saying everything should be inside, or that you should out-source the majority of it."

Regardless, companies will continue to face challenges. And they'll make mistakes. One of the biggest mistakes Imholz sees companies make is "to try to outsource a problem"—in other words, farming out an underperforming element of the IT operation. "That's the wrong way to go about it," he said. "If you can't manage something reasonably well, then you're not going to do terribly well outsourcing it, because the management responsibility doesn't go away." If you're going to outsource a problem, Imholz said, fix it first.

■ ■ ■

Ken Lawler, who worked for years with Imholz at McDonnell Douglas and Boeing, recalled when Imholz convinced company management to switch over from tapes to new storage technologies. They'd used IBM tapes for years, and they worked fine, so why switch? Imholz demon-strated the value that the new offerings could bring, and it led to a 50 percent cost saving.

"Don fought those fights. The management above him respected him so much because of that," Lawler said. "And he did that in a quiet fashion. It's an unusual person who can do that. Most people get up and want to pound their chests."

And he's right. Imholz isn't long-winded. He's certainly not one to pound his chest; in fact, to some degree, he might be humble to a fault.

When he looked back at his career to date, Imholz talked about wishing he had built more relationships. A lot of his shortcoming there, he said, is due to being an introvert. Imholz has a close rela-tionship with Michael Neidorff, Centene's chairman and CEO, who is much more of an extrovert. They could go to dinner with 10 people, and Neidorff will come back with more energy than before. Imholz walks away from a setting like that thinking to himself, "Give me a quiet room for a while so I can recharge."

Imholz also cited one of the biggest compliments he received dur-ing his time in aerospace. He and the CEO of Boeing's defense busi-ness were meeting with a parts supplier. They were looking to expand their relationship with the supplier, first to develop a more collaborative partnership on engineering and manufacturing, with the possibility of an acquisition down the road.

Imholz eventually began leading some of the meetings with the company. At one point, the senior executive from the supplier went to the CEO, asking why an "IT guy" was running the meetings. The Boeing defense CEO told him, "He's as good of a businessperson as I've got."

Now, it's safe to assume that plenty of executives have made similar comments about Imholz, given his track record. But the fact that he was so flattered points to his humble side, which has certainly served him well through his career.

Despite that humility, Imholz knows what he brings to the table, and he knows what his experiences in defense and aerospace did to shape his leadership style.

"It helped solidify my understanding of running IT as a good business and not just being a good technologist," he said. "Those experiences helped round me out as a businessperson. I had the IT skills—vendor management, leadership, financial analysis. The work we did had to do with managing IT, but it was not just about technology."

And he'd seen his fair share of life outside technology. Even before his finance rotations, Imholz had extensive experience in the business. Early in his career, he worked in manufacturing. He dabbled in the engineering side. He immersed himself in program management. He led special projects. And he worked on highly classified areas (so we can't talk about them here).

Roll that up, together with his education, and the introvert had the complete package—and the unimpeachable confidence—to take on a rather unlikely career shift.

■ ■ ■

When Centene first approached Imholz, he was hesitant. Full-time work was not high on his list.

After he agreed to consult and got started with some heavy lifting, Neidorff was one of the many Centene executives working to persuade

Imholz to join as CIO. When Neidorff posed the question, Imholz was flattered, but he had a simple response: "Why me? I know next to nothing about health care."

Neidorff's answer might have sealed the deal in getting the IT leader he wanted. "His reply was twofold," Imholz recalled. "He knew I was going to learn it, but that it would take time, and he already had a lot of people who understood health care. He saw the company getting bigger, and he wanted someone who understood what technology could do for a company like Centene and how to run a large organization."

Imholz remained skeptical—he knew he'd soon have to master the health care lexicon and acronyms—but he was received with open arms. Company leaders understood that Imholz was bringing not IT leadership experience, but big-company business leadership that would be invaluable as Centene tackled new challenges.

And that has played out. Today, Imholz evenly divides his time on three core responsibilities: IT, non-IT, and general management. The one-third he spends on IT involves strategy and big-ticket, long-term issues. He also heads Centene's shared services operation. All of the company's claims operations report up through him. And just by nature of being one of the senior leaders at the company, he's often brought into other corporate initiatives from a general management perspective. "Everything affects IT and operations," Imholz said, "so I'm happy to be involved on the front end."

Imholz firmly believes in multiple channels of communication and never getting constrained by levels of the organization. "Always give direction through the hierarchy, but seek information from anywhere" is the mantra. So as someone who's continuously learning the industry, he likes to meet with groups of new employees. Every month, he randomly pulls people from across the IT organization into a room to talk shop. Imholz answers all the questions he gets, but he said he learns more from the questions than people do from his answers.

When Imholz started out in the aerospace business, he read every industry publication he could find. As he evolved into more senior roles, he incorporated more *Wall Street Journal* and general business and leadership reading, and he continues doing that today. He doesn't read much on aerospace anymore—he's replaced it with energetic research and study of the health care industry.

And it's been quite a learning experience. Looking back at his time in health care so far, Imholz sees plenty of differences from his former industry. The first B-52 made its maiden flight in 1952, and the Air Force projects the bomber will remain operational until at least 2038. That's a rather long product life cycle. There's a saying in the aerospace world that the first B-52 pilots are long in their graves, but the last might not be born yet. "Aerospace companies tend to think and plan capacity looking out, easily, 5, 10, or 15 years," Imholz said. Health care companies, on the other hand, "think ahead to after lunch."

Health care is much more dynamic in terms of changes to service and structure than aerospace, Imholz added. It's a highly fragmented business, but it's also in an exciting period: it's undergoing "cataclysmic change" due to massive overhauls on the legislative and regulatory fronts (think Obamacare).

Cataclysmic change—that's not the first time Imholz has uttered those words, and it's not the first time he's been at the forefront of revolutionary transformation.

Sometimes things really do come full circle.

■ ■ ■

Although Imholz has been around to see game-changing innovations in IT, he's also been building a resume of a versatile, multifaceted IT leader who, among all things, is business-first.

We've all heard the term *CIO-plus* lobbed around to describe an IT leader who has taken on additional responsibilities, and many of the best CIO-plus leaders around are included in this book. What's interesting about Imholz and the others is how they build the know-how throughout their careers to be able to handle those extra responsibilities.

Many CIO-plus leaders gained more responsibilities after rising to the CIO perch. They've defied the old adage, "What got you here won't keep you here," which many use to explain that IT leaders must get away from their own previous IT experience in order to succeed in the C-suite. Business smarts, strategic thinking, building strong, collaborate relationships with executive peers—those are some of the crucial ingredients for success.

Imholz, too, took on more responsibilities after becoming a CIO. But none of it would be possible without what he had done in the past. During his turns in finance, he actually served as a division CFO. He's run service organizations. He speaks Lean and Six Sigma fluently. He's something of the converse of that old adage.

And that matters, too, in the age of the CIO-plus. "Whether you call it shared services or operations, it's recognition that people that are going to be at the table because of IT, if they're going to stay there, it's going to be because they have more than IT experience, and then they're recognized as being able to do other things," Imholz said.

Then there are his own unique attributes. Ken Lawler points to two qualities when describing Imholz's leadership prowess. The first is his integrity—Imholz does things for the right reasons, not political reasons, Lawler said.

The second is somewhat connected. Imholz is objective. According to Lawler, Imholz excels at getting the right people together to examine opportunities and challenges objectively. When it comes to decisions about, say, outsourcing, if the numbers showed that they shouldn't outsource, Imholz would say not to outsource. Plain and simple, and clear, regardless of the political pressure.

"A lot of people want to hear the right answer, not the real answer," Lawler said. "Don wants the real answer."

Imholz's humility is another attribute that's propelled him forward. There was another piece of the conversation with Neidorff, when Centene's CEO was trying to persuade him to join the company: they never discussed compensation.

"It was never about money," Imholz said. "I didn't need to work. If I wanted to work, it would be because I could make a contribution and have some fun.

"Fun for me is taking on challenging situations."

CHAPTER 8

The Accidental CIO: Sheleen Quish

S heleen Quish wasn't a powerful elected official. She wasn't carrying ultrasensitive materials in some silver briefcase.

But for three months during her stint as CIO of Illinois Blue Cross, Sheleen Quish walked between her car and her office with a security detail.

She had received a death threat. And it came from inside her company.

After being recruited by the $4 billion company's CEO, Ray McCaskey, Quish faced an uphill battle as she worked to reshape and reenergize an IT organization that was getting low marks from all over the company. Quish entered the role with significant experience not only in the health care world but also in leading—and overhauling—IT, marketing, and operations departments.

She found in Chicago an organization hostile to change. She found a company hostile to newcomers like her. Perhaps worst of all, she found an executive team that was not 100 percent behind the very person who hired her. He was still proving himself in the CEO role.

She also found a level of political sophistication in Chicago that was vastly different from the easygoing world of Louisville, Kentucky, where she had lived before moving to Chicago. She also found that scaling up to a company four times the size was a more formidable challenge than she had really thought about.

About two years into her tenure, McCaskey summoned Quish to his office. Sitting next to him was the company's chief legal officer, who handed Quish her termination papers.

Like the old days, she was escorted to her car by a security detail. But this time, she had no idea why. Ten years later, she got her answer—and it was one that she never could have imagined.

Quish had logged eight successful years with Southeastern Mutual Insurance Company (Blue Cross Blue Shield of Kentucky), which included oversight of 11 internal divisions, including IT, before coming to Illinois Blue Cross. And despite her unceremonious departure, she racked up quite a few impressive accomplishments in Chicago, to be sure.

Still, she wrestled with a professional existential dilemma: Should she ever pursue another technology leadership role again? It was a difficult question to face, particularly in a time of distress.

It was also an interesting conundrum for someone who, despite years of success as an IT leader, had absolutely zero technical training.

■ ■ ■

Growing up in the Quish household in Manchester, Connecticut, a suburb located 10 miles east of Hartford, politics was an overarching theme. Her parents were fervent about politics—but there was a twist: Dad was an Irish Catholic Democrat, Mom a Protestant Republican.

Quish—the older sister to four brothers—was forced to dabble in both sides of the political debate. Her mother would drag her to the local Republican headquarters, where she made signs and knocked on doors to rally support for candidates. Her dad would host events at the family home for a local Democrat, and since her mother would leave, Quish would serve as the hostess for the arriving crowd.

Her father's family business was serving as the local undertaker. "That whole upbringing—growing up in this small town with your grandfather and father in the same business, and it's a business where you're very sensitive to people—there was always this sense that people were watching you, that you were representing the business," Quish said. "You cannot behave in a way that would prevent people from wanting to do business with us."

It was an important lesson that would stay with her throughout her career. She jokes that during her time as an executive at Kentucky Blue Cross Blue Shield, her kids would ask why she was wearing lipstick to the grocery store. She'd reply, quite simply, that she could run into policyholders or one of the 1,500 employees who could easily recognize her. Just like the undertaking business, the health care world required trust and sensitivity.

Quish's road to her business career was equally as interesting as her career achievements. If her dad would have had it his way, she would have gone to hairdressing school. That way, he wouldn't have to pay someone else to do the hair and makeup on the bodies at the mortuary—she would do it. On top of that, he thought it would be rather enterprising for her to marry a guy from the Italian side of Manchester. Nothing wrong with opening up a whole new market segment, right?

He didn't get his way. The influential women in her life—her mother, grandmother, and godmother—had been pushing her to strive for a college education her whole life.

Quish went off to the College of New Rochelle, a few hours west, where she earned her degree in fine arts. She figured with that degree, she could do anything. "People told me to get a teacher certification to fall back on— 'You know, just in case you don't marry some wealthy man,'" Quish said. "I said no—I will never fall back on anything."

She would push ahead, no matter what. And soon enough—and at some critical times in her career—she would need to.

■ ■ ■

While she was at college, Quish's family hit a rough spot financially. The nuns at her all-women Catholic school never told her that her parents had been paying with bad checks. But finally, in her junior year, they broke the news.

Instead of going nuclear, the nuns told her to go home, talk with her parents, and find a solution. In the middle of the week, she took a train home and sat her parents down. They found a solution—her parents were able to find the needed money, and Quish took out loans and worked—and she was able to move forward.

"What I realized at this point: you'd better just take care of yourself," Quish said. "They're not parents anymore. And I needed to grow up. That was a real wake-up call."

When she earned her degree, Quish had no idea what was next. She knew she couldn't go home—she was done living under her parents' roof. But sometimes adversity ends with opportunity. While she worked through her financial issues, leaders at the college took notice of her. Before she knew it, they hired her as an admissions officer.

For three years in the early 1970s, Quish drove around the country, surviving on $50 per diems and sleep at AAA hotels, talking up the value of an education from a Catholic women's college. The grueling pace and arduous sell—it was the decade of liberation, after all—helped her hone her marketing and public relations chops.

She continued to hone those skills over the next decade or so, first in the nonprofit world and then in the health care arena, an industry she would call home for the next 15 years—and would provide her first opportunity to lead an IT organization.

■ ■ ■

In 1985, Quish joined Southeastern Mutual Insurance Company, more widely known as Blue Cross Blue Shield of Kentucky, as director of marketing. In just four years, she climbed the marketing ladder and moved into operations as a senior vice president.

Right about that time, she cut a deal with the CFO who had been managing IT and found them a difficult, recalcitrant group to lead. She volunteered to take over the IT organization, and he happily handed it over. That department was in some disarray. As Quish recalled, IT was a silo with no major connection to the business. For the IT team, the business was a nuisance that got in the way of producing results. "I saw IT as an important toolbox I needed to use to accomplish process reengineering," Quish said. "Every single path led somehow through IT, and every single major process improvement in operations was generally blockaded by the inability of IT to play. They didn't want to play. No one forced them to play."

Her first mission in repairing the organization was to hire a day-to-day leader. She found Solon Young, a systems development whiz from American Airlines' Sabre division, and was determined to get him on the team. It turned out that she would have to pay him more than she was earning. Quish's boss ultimately adjusted Quish's compensation, but Quish insists she would do whatever it took, regardless of whether she profited from it personally.

Young had the infrastructure side covered, but he convinced Quish that they needed to take a page from Sabre and invest more heavily in the development side of the house, including strong R&D. They hired Frank Schlier, who eventually became CIO at Kentucky Blue Cross, a technology executive, and a distinguished analyst at Gartner.

Young and Schlier were just the type of talent Quish needed to turn IT on its head. And it worked. (Sadly, Young died of a heart attack before the age of 40, just a few years into his role there.)

Quish rose to executive vice president and oversaw 11 divisions of the company by the time it was acquired by Anthem in 1992. She also had three subsidiary businesses reporting into her: an electronic database for claims, a third-party administrator, and a data-center services company. By the time she left, Quish had helped reduce operating costs by 12 percent and the head count by 20 percent, along with a 40 percent drop in customer inquiries in an 18-month period. Her reshaped, reenergized IT organization implemented electronic publishing, data warehousing, and EDI functionality in the late 1980s and early 1990s.

Anthem offered her a position that narrowed her scope, so she decided to look elsewhere. That's when a headhunter approached her about a position where he thought she'd be a perfect fit: CIO of Illinois Blue Cross.

■ ■ ■

The headhunter had a point. On paper, Quish was an excellent candidate. In her mind, though, she wasn't sold.

But she flew to Chicago to meet with McCaskey, who told her he agreed with the headhunter's assessment. Quish liked what she was hearing, and she was intrigued about the idea of such a prominent role with a multibillion-dollar company.

Illinois Blue Cross had never had a CIO, McCaskey explained, and Quish's crossover between IT and operations would be a great fit. And, of course, Quish could be a good backup if operations would ever need a caretaker.

He also thought Quish could make an impact in overseeing administration, which included purchasing facilities and equipment. The company's lease at Illinois Center, a large mixed-use complex in Chicago's Loop, was coming up. Quish would lead a project to find new land on which to build a new headquarters—an initiative that would involve the CEO and board of directors.

McCaskey himself was new to the role. He had been a peer to those he was now overseeing, and as Quish recalled, there was a considerable amount of tension within the executive ranks about his appointment to the top spot. But he had grand plans to retool his executive team, and Quish was the first new kid on the block.

But despite the reach she was entrusted with, IT was definitely the first priority. McCaskey told Quish about the mess he had on his hands. They had big projects coming up, but the organization wasn't functioning the way it could be. Internally, no one was happy with IT's performance, Quish learned. When she eventually did a side-by-side analysis of her new unit against her department in Kentucky, she saw glaring problems. Too much silo mentality. The infrastructure and development teams didn't communicate. Nothing was truly integrated with the overall business strategy.

Too much money was being poured into a problem department. It needed a total transformation.

Quish took the job, and she started on her transformation with two initial ideas. The first was to hire a technical advisor. She felt this was necessary to fill her technical gaps and provide the objective counterpoint to the old guard in IT who felt that everything was fine the way it was.

The second was to bring in the marketing firm she used in Kentucky, whose people she trusted. The IT organization needed a full-tilt rebranding—not only to promote its capability externally but also to boost confidence and dedication internally. As Quish said, the team needed a "whole new life" in terms of its purpose, mission, structure, and relationship with the business.

But convincing the IT organization that it had a problem was no easy task.

■ ■ ■

Quish brought in a research company that surveyed Illinois Blue Cross's business units to get their feedback on the IT organization. The results were "devastating," Quish recalled. But since she was so new, she didn't think IT would respond well if she delivered the news. "No one in IT would believe me," she said. "On the business side, the executive team probably would have believed it, but it wouldn't have mattered—if IT didn't believe it, they would never change."

So she took a different tack. She would call her 400 IT employees together for a town hall meeting, but she turned to Second City, Chicago's renowned comedy troupe, to add some levity to the room.

In a hotel ballroom in downtown Chicago, representatives from the research firm detailed the methodologies and confidentiality disclaimers attached to their report. They hit the right notes in terms of tech-speak, so Quish thought her team was dialed in.

Then came the actual results. As the research team painted the horrific perception of the IT organization, players from Second City began reacting. "What the hell? I can't believe it!" "I know, it's all my fault!" They started jumping up, walking down the aisles, storming out of the ballroom. None of the IT team members knew that the actors were planted, so there was some real shock value. "We had all these different reactions," Quish said, "and they were so realistic." Just as some of the IT folks began thinking it was a ruse, the Second City team jumped on stage and performed a sketch with a little song and dance.

Once the performance ended, Quish took over. They knew the current state of things, but now they had to focus on what came next. To her, it was about change—more accurately, the desperate need for change.

She unveiled a new logo for the department. She explained their new mission. She detailed how they would better interact with the business to drive results—and drive down the disapproval ratings.

From there, Quish brought in new project managers, many of whom came from big accounting firms armed with the credibility to manage and enforce new processes. She launched a newsletter that not only communicated changes to IT but also introduced the "new" IT department to the rest of the organization.

The immediate feedback split both ways. A good chunk of her employees got on board—they liked her approach, and they got reenergized about their work. But Quish said there was also a core group that formed a united front against her. "To my face, they were very nice," Quish said. "Behind my back, they were bitching and moaning and groaning. They were really, really angry about it."

■ ■ ■

The death threat came pretty soon after that. It was a male voice on her answering machine at work, but the message was clear: If she kept doing what she was doing, she'd end up dead. (To this day, Quish does not know who left the message.)

Quish kept moving forward, determined to finish what she started. And a funny thing happened: the IT organization really started clicking. Production was up. Quality was up. They were tackling big projects and growing their reputation across the company.

Along the way, Quish was living the life in Chicago. In 1993, her first year with the company, the Chicago Bulls won their third-straight National Basketball Association championship, crowning Michael Jordan as perhaps the best player in league history. Quish basked in the glory from choice playoff-game seats. Vendors wined and dined her. She oversaw the construction of the new headquarters building, and Mayor Richard M. Daley was on hand for the groundbreaking.

Her family told Quish her head was getting pretty big. That changed pretty quickly.

When she got the call to go to McCaskey's office, she didn't know what would happen. When she saw the general counsel there, too, she still didn't know, but she wasn't expecting anything too bad.

Within minutes, she got her walking papers. Her termination letter didn't include a cause. She got full severance, and for a year she would keep her benefits and company car, along with getting outplacement services. Before the security guards whisked her out of the building, she asked why she was being fired. No answer.

What went wrong? That was the question Quish would ask herself after that fateful meeting. Indeed, her confidence was up, but not to the point where she wouldn't see this coming. Or so she thought.

After some reflection, Quish arrived at a logical conclusion: she hadn't built the right relationships with her peers in the C-suite. It was certainly a tough row to hoe. McCaskey kept telling her not to worry about certain executives, because chances were they would be out the door soon as he sought to reshape the leadership lineup. Looking back, Quish thought that maybe she hadn't given her usual 100 percent to building the right rapport with them. That backfired, because those executives had too much clout and strong relationships with the board—they weren't going anywhere, despite McCaskey's assurances.

She kept telling herself that that's where she went wrong. The internal politics were complex and cutthroat—this was Chicago, after all—and Quish read the tea leaves wrong.

After she got past the shock of her firing, she went about networking and working with the outplacement service to find her next role. Quish was so aggressive, in fact, that the outplacement team told her to go home and take a breather. But she wasn't sitting back—at the time, she was a single mother of two kids, and she also had her mother living with them in Chicago.

Then there was the dilemma of whether she would continue down the CIO path. Quish was battle-tested—in her upbringing and her business career—and she had developed a pretty thick skin as a female business executive, thanks to the strong women who had influenced her life.

But the question remained.

■ ■ ■

Despite the fallout, Quish would occasionally bump into former colleagues at Illinois Blue Cross. Lower-level employees would tell Quish they missed her. Her administrative assistant continues to this day to send birthday and holiday cards. "It was nice to know *someone* liked me," Quish said.

While Quish deliberated her future, she received an interesting proposal. Deborah Bricker, the owner of Bricker Consulting, who had successfully supported some key projects in IT at Illinois Blue Cross, approached Quish and said she thought Quish would make a great partner in her flourishing enterprise.

Quish didn't want to be a consultant. She told Bricker; Bricker said she already knew that. But why not come in and do some fun work while you look for another job? Bricker asked. She agreed to pay Quish the same salary she had been making at Illinois Blue Cross, so Quish decided to give it a go.

For the next year, she worked on projects with an assortment of different organizations in a variety of industries. Along the way, she regained her swagger—and her interest in information technology leadership.

From there, she moved on to Signature Group as EVP of corporate planning and information services. Next came a two-year stint as

SVP of insurance operations and information technology at Unitrin. Then she took the global CIO role at U.S. Can, where she stayed for five years until the company was acquired by Ball Corporation in 2005.

Afterward, Quish hung out her own shingle, forming Box 9 Consulting out of Chicago. Plenty of CIOs do consulting work between jobs, and Quish quickly began working on projects with companies across multiple sectors and industries.

In late 2006, Quish got a call from Martha Heller, a CIO headhunter who went on to start an eponymous executive search firm. Heller first came across Quish when she was writing a column for *CIO* magazine about how CIOs can brand themselves. She was blown away by Quish's background and perspectives.

Heller was handling the search for a CIO for Ameristar Casinos in Las Vegas. She had been in touch with Quish early on in the search process—mainly probing her for recommendations from her vast Rolodex. After speaking further with Ameristar's President John Boushy, Heller had an idea.

"The whole time, I was thinking John would really love Sheleen," Heller said. "[Boushy] was in marketing and IT; Sheleen was in marketing and IT. Executive search is a lot like matchmaking."

But Quish wasn't catching on. She had no industry experience, so she didn't think she'd be a viable candidate. Plus, she had just relocated and bought a beautiful home on Lake Michigan.

Heller persisted, and Quish ultimately came up with an alternative idea: Quish should come in as interim CIO for a few months. Heller introduced Boushy and Quish by phone. They spoke for several hours, Heller said, and Boushy "fell in love with her."

Quish took the job as interim CIO in January 2007. Just four months later, the company pulled the "interim" tag.

■ ■ ■

For many business leaders, it takes time to get fully acclimated in a new corporate environment. In her roles at Blue Crosses in Kentucky and Illinois, she had to jump right in. But now she was an interim CIO, with an expectation of staying on board for a few months. Her top priorities were to stabilize the existing IT operation and find a new, permanent CIO to lead it.

And it wasn't an easy culture to blend into. Just like at Illinois Blue Cross, she was the new arrival on a leadership team that had logged years at the firm and embodied the founder's vision for the company, Heller recalled. "You can be great at operations and process, but there's a *je ne sais quoi* that some executives have where they can communicate with people and have people know that she is listening and that she cares," Heller said of Quish. "I'm confident that part of Sheleen's confidence and success was that she had [the whole package]."

About six weeks into her interim assignment at Ameristar, Quish put together a laundry list of problems she saw in the IT organization. Quoting a board member's comment five years later, Quish found "a pile of garbage."

"I wasn't just a caretaker CIO," Quish said. "I came in all guns blasting."

Ameristar's IT shop hadn't done any major systems maintenance for years. When daylight savings time came, the IT team made all adjustments manually. There was no process, so it almost crippled the company.

Ameristar operated seven casino properties in six states, and those properties did whatever they wanted with IT. The corporate IT organization had little to do with any of those decisions. They had spent $3 million trying to implement a universal loyalty card that would link all the casino properties together but had literally nothing to show for it. It was complete chaos.

In Quish's eyes, no one wanted to truly manage IT. Except for her.

So she pitched the idea of building a true enterprise IT organization that would govern the properties. Her message to the general managers: Let me handle IT—you focus on your guests and your operations. Letting each casino run its own fiefdom was risky, particularly with the high degree of regulation enforced by gaming commissions. The GMs agreed, as did Ameristar's corporate leadership.

But then came the harder part: selling her plan to the casino IT directors. Those folks had it good. They essentially had autonomy to do whatever they wanted, and without a strong, centralized IT organization, they were accountable to no one. Their world, their silo.

Now they had the hard-charging Quish as corporate CIO. She delivered a clear edict. "I basically said, 'This is the business model we're following. This is what you used to do, this is what we're going to do, and here's how we're going to get there,'" Quish said. "'Either you're with me or you're not. You make your decision, because I'm not changing my model.'"

■ ■ ■

That snapshot is one of the best encapsulations of Quish as a business leader. She identified the problem, set a clear vision of how to fix it, and got the buy-in she needed from corporate leadership. Here was a seasoned executive—who had fought her fair share of battles—making the decisions that true leaders make.

It's also part of the irony of Quish's career. "When I think about it, it was an accidental process," Quish said. "I did not aspire to become a CIO. I call myself the 'Accidental CIO' because it wasn't a career path I had planned out. I have no technical background at all."

When she delivered the mandate to the IT directors, some of them balked. Staying firm, Quish replaced them with new talent who got in line with her vision. She focused on team building to strengthen the new enterprise IT organization, and she was getting results. So much so, that, five years later, when Pinnacle Entertainment announced plans to buy Ameristar Casinos, the first thing the IT directors said was "Don't undo our model! Don't make me take that stuff back!"

The merger catapulted Quish into a brand new role: serving as Ameristar's lead in integrating with Pinnacle. Quish had already been elevated to lead human resources at Ameristar, in addition to IT, and this new role called on not only her expertise in those functions but also her past experience in operations and marketing.

After the acquisition was announced, representatives from Pinnacle and Ameristar began holding "discovery" meetings that outlined how both sides did business and how they would do business as a merged entity. During those 21 meetings, Quish began to see many of the challenges ahead.

Pinnacle was much more decentralized than Ameristar. In their operating regions, managers had tremendous autonomy. The same went for their IT and marketing operations. It was the same problems—and challenges—Quish had seen before.

When the issue of planning and analysis came up at the discovery meetings, Quish listened as Pinnacle staff outlined their processes. As Pinnacle boasted about their budget and dashboard capabilities, Quish had a bit of déjà vu.

In 2011, Ameristar embraced a data warehouse solution out of necessity. A leader in the company's financial planning and analysis group came to her with the request. He didn't really know anything about data warehouses, but he knew he needed one. Quish and her team coached him through the technical particulars, and two years later, he had built what Quish called the best analytics group in the industry.

In the process, she had to collaborate closely with all sides of Ameristar—not only planning and analytics but also marketing and operations. Better data meant better decisions. And since Ameristar was so far ahead of Pinnacle, it was yet another past success that would help make the combined company even stronger.

All throughout the process, Quish harkened back to her upbringing, recalling how important it was to represent the business. In addition, she took a few pages from her successes in communicating her vision to her teams and then marketing those visions to the rest of the business.

She knew that plenty of employees would be nervous about the merger, their own futures, and possible cultural changes that could take place. "People watch us as executives; if I look terrified or frightened, they're going to read into it and start asking, 'What's wrong?' or 'What's about to happen?'" Quish said. "For the merger, we talked about it honestly and transparently from the get-go. We said it was the marriage of two strong companies that are only going to get better together."

■ ■ ■

Although Quish no longer served as the CIO of Ameristar, the function reported to her. In September 2013, after feeling confident in the progress of the integration, Quish decided to step away, opting to pursue more opportunities to write, speak, and consult.

But of all the functional leadership roles she had tackled, the most curious of all might have been her other departmental responsibility at Ameristar: human resources.

It's not every day that a CIO takes on HR as an additional responsibility. Heading a development department, shared services, supply chain, or even operations tends to be a more traditional extra role for a CIO-plus. In fact, you can probably count on one hand the number of CIOs at medium or large businesses who have also overseen HR.

In January 2011, she did just that.

According to Heller, leaders at Ameristar took notice—early— how Quish was successfully staffing her IT organization. She brought in talented professionals from outside the industry. She started different practices, like rewarding her team members for outstanding work. And she focused on innovation, not operation. "Usually, IT is trying to catch up with culture, and here, Sheleen was building the kind of culture that other departments wanted to emulate," Heller said.

In the official announcement, Ameristar President and COO Larry Hodges summed up the move to her unique mix of skills. "Sheleen is a change driver," Hodges said in the press release. "Sheleen sets aggressive goals and produces measurable results. Her ability to align people, processes and technology to achieve outstanding outcomes and business objectives made her the obvious choice. . . . This dual role will allow her to shape integrated, result-oriented and profit-focused teams in every department."

Quish sees clear overlap. In addition to being two functions that have their own language and policies, they also follow processes by the book. And because they share a lineage as order-taker cultures, the processes of transforming them into more value-adding operations are quite similar.

Just like she wasn't afraid to take on IT back in Louisville, she didn't hesitate to take on HR in Las Vegas. And the intersection proved to be very apropos in 2013, when Quish set out to tackle her primary problem at Ameristar.

Her mission was to develop a new scheduling method for staffing the casinos. Ameristar had 7,000 full-time employees across its eight properties. But in the casino business, about 60 percent of revenue comes in over a 36-hour period over the weekend.

Ameristar morphed its workforce into more part-time than full-time, giving them flexibility to handle the higher-volume periods. But recruiting and retaining part-time staff would pose challenges. Ameristar made the mistake of telling employees when they had to work, as opposed to trying to work with their best availability. Quish knew a thing or two about work-life balance and thought there could be a better approach.

So Quish changed the mentality. Instead of ordering them to work a shift, Ameristar would collaborate with its employees to create the right schedules—and provide online access to make changes to their schedules. The people part of it was taken care of.

But scheduling was still done manually, for the most part, and it was very political on the casino level. So Quish put on her CIO hat and partnered with business leaders to find an automated system that made scheduling both more efficient and more democratic. The technology side of the issue was resolved.

And on top of that, it quelled the company's turnover issues, and it actually led to a significant bump in EBITDA from day one. She said the EBITDA gains could be even higher if they could optimize their process even further.

There was just enough sensitivity from the personnel and technological fronts that it could have been an even bigger problem. It took a unique leader—who speaks and thinks business first—to make that kind of measurable impact on what many would see as a routine or minor issue.

■ ■ ■

Ten years after she was fired by Illinois Blue Cross, Quish finally learned why.

The operations executive Quish had worked with called her out of the blue. The executive asked Quish to get together for a drink in Chicago. Quish agreed—she was always networking, so she didn't think it was anything more than that. When they met up, they engaged in a conversation that Quish had waited a decade for, although she had no idea who would be on the other side.

Colleague: Do you ever wonder what happened, why you were terminated?

Quish: I know. I figured it out. I did a terrible job building relationships. It's changed the way I operate.

Colleague: No, not really.

Quish: What do you mean?

Colleague: I'm the reason you were terminated.

Quish: What do you mean? I thought you liked me.

Colleague: It had nothing to do with you.

Quish: Well, how did you get IT back under you?

Colleague: I was approached by another Blue Cross company about opportunities with them, and they included IT. I went to the [Illinois Blue Cross] CEO, and he matched the deal.

According to Quish, this executive had been with the company for 30 years. There were tight relationships with the board, and it would have been impossible to explain her departure.

Colleague: So, you had to go.

Quish: Wow. I would have worked for you.

In all of her endeavors since Illinois Blue Cross, Quish had worked tirelessly to build strong relationships with her executive peers. She had continuously pushed forward, driven by her analysis of her mistakes there—and the determination to never make them again.

This colleague had just turned a decade's worth of action on its head.

Quish thought back to her recruitment to Illinois Blue Cross. How Realtors had fallen all over themselves to accommodate her. How this big company had said all the right things.

She thought back to her high-flying days in Chicago. How her head had gotten too big for her body.

And she thought back to her firing. How she had learned that Chicago was a town of not only governmental politics but office politics as well.

Quish quickly made peace with the shock just delivered to her system. This colleague might have been telling the absolute truth, but reflecting back, Quish still shoulders the blame. "The real lesson learned: I didn't build the relationships the right way," Quish said. "There's no excuse."

She thought about another important lesson she learned from that difficult event: humility. In another world, Quish might have been the best hairdresser Manchester, Connecticut, had ever seen.

CHAPTER 9

The Innovator: Greg Schwartz

t was 5 o'clock on a warm July 2012 morning in San Antonio when 300 people came into formation on a soccer field. The forecast called for a 93-degree day.

Drill sergeants were there, eager to break in the new recruits. Push-ups. Sit-ups. Calisthenics. Orders barked at the highest volumes.

The workout ended with a mile-and-a-half run. At the conclusion, Greg Schwartz couldn't even lift his arms.

But this wasn't boot camp. Well, maybe it was. The 300 trainees weren't new recruits to the armed forces—they were IT professionals. The drill sergeants were retired from active duty. All were employees at USAA.

The arm-weary Schwartz had been the company's CIO since 2004. He sponsored the boot-camp program—called Zero-Day PT—in 2009 as a way to train his own people to understand just who USAA serves. "You learn about the military. You learn about what our members go through so you can better appreciate what you do every single day," Schwartz said. "It brings them closer to our mission."

That mission, as Schwartz explained, is to provide a customer service experience unparalleled in the financial services industry. USAA earned more than $20 billion in revenue in its 2012 fiscal year by providing banking, investing, and insurance to U.S. service members and their families. And over the years, USAA has racked up numerous accolades for keeping its customers happy. Whether in a combat zone or back on U.S. soil, USAA members—the soldiers, sailors, Marines, airmen, and their families are not customers, they're "members"—can access the company's services via the web or mobile applications.

But it wasn't always that way.

When Schwartz took over as CIO, the first order of business for himself and his team was to reach out to USAA's business-line chiefs to gauge their perspective on the company's IT operation.

This was early in the Internet age, and the feedback they received wasn't much different than what most IT organizations heard at the time. In other words, it wasn't great.

Speaking in July 2013, on the very day USAA received its fourth straight plaque from *Computerworld*'s "100 Best Places to Work in IT" awards—they had been ranked No. 1 the past three years and ranked No. 1 for large companies (No. 2 overall) in 2013—Schwartz recounted what he heard from those business units a decade earlier.

USAA's IT organization was good—that was clear. But they weren't transparent enough. Even more important, they cost too much. They took too long to deliver. And they were nowhere near as innovative as their business partners needed them to be.

That was the perception. "I use the word *perception* because part of it was real, and part of it not so real," Schwartz said during the interview.

The journey between hearing that feedback and rising to a best-in-class IT organization was an uphill battle that even the best military leaders couldn't script.

■ ■ ■

Each day, USAA employees walk into the corporate campus in San Antonio, Texas, unfazed by its enormity. The main building, which contains 4.2 million square feet, sits on 282 acres. If you turned the Willis Tower (still known to most as the Sears Tower) on its side, the USAA building would be longer.

The facility, built over an old horse farm, is known as the McDermott Building. Given its size, it's a humble moniker for its namesake. Robert McDermott, who had retired as a brigadier general in the U.S. Air Force before becoming chairman and CEO of USAA, also served as the first permanent dean of the faculty at the U.S. Air Force Academy and is widely regarded as the "father of modern military education."

In 1922, USAA was formed by a group of 25 Army officers who pooled money together to insure one another's automobiles. No one else would insure them. In the wake of World War I, military members were just too much of a risk to other insurance companies. When

USAA employees enter the lobby of the McDermott Building, they're greeted by large WWI-era portraits, reminding them not only of the company's origin, but who exactly they serve.

USAA offered automobile insurance, later adding life and homeowner's policies, as well as bank and brokerage services. All the while, their business grew not through local agents but via the phone and mail. In 1999, the company launched its online service.

Innovative in and of itself, USAA was known for decades as a pioneer on both the customer-service and technological fronts. They hit it big in 1988 with Image Plus, an image-processing system that scans and stores all policy information received by mail. The system was also marketed by IBM, which codeveloped it with USAA.

In more recent memory, anyone who watches TV remembers the onslaught of ads by Chase in 2010 touting its check-scanning smartphone application. USAA released its Deposit@Mobile app a year earlier. It was based on the Deposit@Home customer offering it had launched in 2006, allowing customers to scan their own checks and submit the images to USAA to deposit into their accounts.

Schwartz was in the building for all these innovations. He joined USAA after earning his undergraduate degree in management information systems from Texas State University in 1982, and he's been there ever since.

The check-scanning app happened under his watch, but Schwartz attributes the success of that innovation to his team and their collaboration with business partners. Since becoming CIO, part of Schwartz's plan has been to inspire passion and reignite that innovative prowess—and to respond to the rest of the concerns voiced by USAA's business leaders.

He set out to improve not only innovation but also three other key areas: running his organization like a business, operating with excellence, and building a stronger, higher-performing workforce.

■ ■ ■

"Run IT like a business." Most IT leaders cringe when they hear that expression today, and Schwartz is the first to admit that.

But back in 2004, it was one of the more oft-used phrases from other functional business leaders when describing exactly what CIOs needed to do to gain more respect. Schwartz had heard the same demand several years earlier, when he led the company's planning and architecture group.

At that time, USAA's IT organization was a chargeback-based operation. If IT was dealing with Joe Robles, USAA's current CEO, who was the chief financial officer at the time, IT's expenses for services provided to the unit would be allocated from Robles's budget. The problem was, all those costs were lumped together, and the business-line leaders had little control over their IT spend. So Schwartz set out to create more cost transparency for his internal customers.

In six months' time, his team deployed a new activity-based accounting system. To this day, everyone in the IT organization—including Schwartz—completes a weekly timesheet that accounts for all activities. That way, his team can charge back different departments for services rendered based on their consumption or their volume.

At the same time, Schwartz's team initiated a new product catalog aimed at making it easier for internal customers to understand what they were buying from IT. Overall, Schwartz's organization supports about 2,500 applications—but reading 2,500 line items on a bill was untenable. So they worked with the business units and regrouped everything into 125 critical systems headings. Within those were eight core products—think computers, mobile devices, and so on.

Getting the billing model under control was what Schwartz called the "run-the-business" piece of his budget. And it allowed IT leaders to focus more heavily on the other part, the one that gets him more excited: "Change the business."

To change the business, they needed operational improvement. Streamlining the cost model helped them move in the right direction.

From that point on, when the business units consumed those core products, they saw it on their bill. Schwartz and his team would sit down with business leaders and show them, year over year, how their costs were going up or down. And they could talk with the business leaders about how they could reduce those costs—and chart the course for improvements in productivity and functionality.

An added bonus was the improvement in inventory control. If the senior financial officer (USAA's name for IT's top finance executive, otherwise known as the CFO) has 150 people in his organization and 200 desktops that he is being charged for, Schwartz can help him see the need to shave costs by returning those resources. When the senior financial officer turns in those machines, Schwartz's team immediately takes them off the tab.

When Schwartz started out as CIO, about 70 percent of USAA's IT budget—not unlike the rest of the financial services industry—went to run-the-business activity. Today, more than half of Schwartz's budget goes to the change-the-business side of the mission.

■ ■ ■

Before you can operate with excellence, you have to have your house in order. The billing improvements Schwartz and his team initiated gave the IT organization the tools they needed to better understand costs and build transparency and credibility with customers—simply put, to run better.

Today, Schwartz is responsible for a budget of more than $1 billion. Repeatability is essential, given that almost half of that budget involves ongoing projects. That's where operational excellence comes in—for every dollar invested in IT, Schwartz needs to give a predictable return of when those projects will come to fruition and add value to internal business customers.

For that and other key metrics, Schwartz and his team have created dashboards that keep the spirit of transparency flowing. His direct reports, who own the key processes of interacting with the business, share them with business partners as often as weekly. Beyond that, the dashboards give Schwartz's organization a clear view of their performance—and help them set targets to shoot for.

Schwartz tracks 20 key metrics overall. Two of them stand out, both from an operational perspective and for customer satisfaction purposes. The first is simple: availability. "That is our lifeblood—90 percent of our interactions with customers are electronic today," Schwartz said. (And of those electronic interactions, more than half were accessed by mobile devices, beginning in December 2012.)

The second is more interesting. Schwartz calls it the "pain" metric.

In this day and age, the majority of people reading this book interact with their bank in one form or another—it could be checking your balance online, transferring funds via smartphone, or live-chatting with a customer service representative.

Now, think about outages. Think about when you've gone to the bank's site and all you've gotten was a vague or unintelligible message saying it can't process your transaction. Then try to quantify the time you've essentially wasted trying to get the service you expect.

Schwartz calls that "pain"—and he's actually quantified it.

Every outage USAA incurs gets a number attached to it: if it's totally gone, it's a 1; if it's a slowdown, it's a 0.5. So think about the soldier, sailor, Marine, or airman who's checking his or her account balance on Monday at 9 A.M. According to volumes across its various channels, USAA often sees 1.5 million service members doing so at that time. If USAA has outages of 30 minutes, Schwartz multiplies those minutes times the number of members affected, and he gets 45 million "pain minutes."

In 2012, USAA members incurred only 5 million or so pain minutes. For 2013, Schwartz's team set a goal of no more than 2 million. As of late July 2013, his team was slightly behind the pace.

But looking at it from a proportional standpoint—volumes had increased from the previous year—they were making solid progress. Back in 2002, USAA averaged about 1.5 pain minutes per member per week. As of July 2013, that statistic was knocked down to about 0.006 of one second. But Schwartz and his team still aren't satisfied.

■ ■ ■

That's an operations example. Schwartz puts as much weight on delivery.

He has eight metrics that his team reviews with internal customers each month and each quarter: projects delivered to cost, projects delivered on schedule, estimating accuracy, scope delivered, benefits, time to market, quality, and productivity.

When USAA benchmarked its project delivery performance against the financial services industry in 2008, competitors were at

231 days with time to market. USAA stood at 201 days. Although it benchmarked well, Schwartz and his team recognized there was still plenty of room for improvement and made this measure a priority moving forward. At the end of 2013, he expects to be at 106. By the time 2016 rolls around, he plans to be at 90 days—all thanks to his partnership with Jim Kuhn, a senior vice president who has led the project delivery group since 2008.

Again, it's about process discipline. "It's absolutely paramount," Schwartz said. When he talks to budding CIOs, he gets a lot of questions about innovation. His take: innovation for innovation's sake doesn't mean much if the operational discipline isn't there. It's all about executing.

And from an execution standpoint, Schwartz sees another area for improvement. By 2018, he wants availability to hit 100 percent. It's a goal that's beyond bold—some would call it unreasonable—but he turns to various investments USAA has made to take them there.

One involves logic. If a system or application crashes overnight, he expects his team to fix it. But he also understands the strain they endure during the workday. So USAA launched what Schwartz calls an "availability command center"—a 24/7 operation staffed by USAA employees and contractors. In 2009, USAA stood up a component of that operation in India. Now USAA has around-the-clock coverage for monitoring systems and resolving any service disruptions quickly. Establishing a center in the opposite hemisphere also helped relieve on-call responsibility for employees in the United States.

The other involves creativity. Humans can take incoming calls about problems or issues with service and respond accordingly. And teams can devote all their time to monitoring uptime, but sometimes you just need a little help.

So Schwartz's team contracted with a third-party service that pings USAA's website every three minutes from 15 locations around the globe. It's a synthetic transaction for a bank, brokerage, and credit card that comes calling, essentially asking, "Hello? Are you there? Can you service my request?"

That same service provider works with other financial services companies, so USAA can see how the company stacks up. For bank and credit card services, USAA has been No. 1 for uptime for the past five years. "For a company that's not brick and mortar," he said, "this is our lifeblood."

Again, there are dashboards for everything—and some of those dashboards get briefed to USAA's board of directors. Schwartz sees them as evidence of the success he and his team had in instilling process discipline into his organization.

All these improvements helped Schwartz focus more heavily on the innovative swagger his department needed to regain. Yes, there was a perception among business leaders that IT wasn't introducing new capabilities or tools to further the business, but that wasn't an absolute fact. Still, Schwartz and his team had work to do.

It's important, first, to understand USAA's philosophy on innovation. He boils it down to a simple statement: innovation, in his words, is any change that adds value. "Think about that for a minute. If that's your definition, then every employee can participate," he said. "They don't have to be in the research and delivery group [only]."

That perspective foreshadowed some of the important initiatives they put in place—and how they envisioned those initiatives becoming realities.

The recalibration on innovation really began before he took the helm as CIO, when he was still a high-ranking IT leader at the company. In 1999, USAA opened its first applied research lab. At that time, emerging technologies were springing up constantly, alongside the explosion of Internet capabilities, and USAA's IT team needed the ability to analyze the changing marketplace—and react.

Creating white papers was one thing, but USAA needed more. So they used the lab to prototype new capabilities and figure out how to sell them to their internal business customers.

A few short years later, USAA made a major breakthrough in banking customer service. Remember, it's mostly a virtual company—with the exception of the single traditional bank location on the San Antonio headquarters campus, there's no branch anywhere in the United States—so most members had always made their bank deposits with USAA by mail. And in that technological era, mail had become another pain metric: members simply didn't want to send in a check. This was a major barrier USAA had to overcome if it was to grow its banking business. So USAA used the applied research lab to develop the home-scanning, remote-deposit capability, which it called Deposit@Home. As more members took to mobile devices, Schwartz and a cross-functional USAA team developed the remote-deposit capture application for smartphones.

All the while, they worked on a problem many IT organizations face with innovation. You can plug away with experiments all day and night, but what happens when you discover a new asset that needs to be delivered quickly?

Schwartz, along with Rickey Burks, USAA's chief technology and innovation officer, proposed a new model they dubbed "Rev Dev," a completely separate funding mechanism that would give their teams the resources to take these new capabilities to production quickly while still experimenting with the more nascent possibilities. With the company's track record for innovation success, senior leaders quickly embraced the idea and approved the funds to make it happen.

Schwartz and Burks were happy with the process and funding changes that built on the culture Schwartz and Burks had developed over the previous two years.

A couple of years earlier, USAA's innovation team had introduced a platform they called ICE (innovation communities for the enterprise). It's essentially a portal through which USAA employees can suggest new ideas—about processes, technical changes, whatever—and vote on the ideas presented. Employees can tag the ones they like (think of it as hitting *Like* on Facebook), and the most popular get moved up the list. Those ideas then go to a group of innovators, who are employees across the different business units who look for optimal ways to deploy the prospective improvements. All the while, a select group of IT employees continues to mine the list—Schwartz's team called it "ICE mining"—for sharp ideas that can help solve existing problems.

Then Schwartz and Burks took it a step further. You've heard of hackathons and innovation tournaments. They decided to employ a similar tack with the suggestions in the ICE platform; they launched a competition called "Code as ICE" that encourages employees to build prototypes of ideas they view as promising.

These competitions now occur quarterly, and employees participate on a voluntary basis. In each competition, there could be as many as 20 five-member, cross-functional teams working on prototypes. They have only 250 hours to finish, and they have to sell their ideas via presentations and videos.

Schwartz said the response was so overwhelming—"We were absolutely floored"—that he had to limit participation. But they got results. The next generation of the remote-deposit capture app came out of this contest, as did an accident re-creation model app for the iPad and a smartphone app for insurance claims.

"Again, it's just another way to get your workforce to embrace the mission," Schwartz said. "It's something that newer employees just love. It works for us, and it works for them."

■ ■ ■

Schwartz's organization looked more like a business. They were operating on a higher plane than before. And the innovation engine was cranking. But all along the way, they were also making improvements on what he called the most core component in bolstering his IT shop: people.

"One of the things I constantly try to impart to my organization and my peers is that people make the difference," he said. "I have a chance to talk to a lot of emerging leaders in IT, and I tell them, it's fun to talk about all these emerging technologies, but people matter most."

Remember, this is an organization that has been hailed—unprecedentedly—as one of the best IT workplaces for four consecutive years. But when he started out as CIO, Schwartz saw opportunities to improve, particularly in growing the number of hires right out of college. And still, despite all the growth, he also needed a variable component to his workforce that could scale up and down rapidly to handle demand.

For college hires, USAA revved up its campus recruiting efforts. This was critical to Schwartz—he was, after all, hired by the company straight out of college. In the summer of 2013, he had 175 college interns from more than 40 universities working in USAA's mammoth office.

The college intern program fuels the college hiring program. USAA brings in interns during their sophomore and junior years; the strategy is, essentially, get them in early and often.

But more important is the message. "We come with the following value proposition: 'We don't want you to just come work for us—we want you to build a career with us,'" Schwartz said. "We are about selling them a career, not just a job."

The variable component was a bit more complicated. When companies look to outsource or offshore IT, they tend to ask the same opening question: What's core to our portfolio, and what isn't?

Schwartz and his team didn't like that approach, and he humbly explained why: Simply put, they didn't feel the organization was prescient enough to determine what would be core and noncore going forward. For example, if you asked him 10 years ago if mainframes were going to go away, he would say yes. Today, he'll tell you absolutely not. On top of that was the fact that USAA was "absolutely vigiliant" about securing its members' information, so that concern added complexity to any resourcing decision.

So, instead of one full-tilt contract with one vendor, Schwartz and his team selectively decided to spread out his needs across four vendors. He does his best to regularly visit them—he visited his supplier in Guadalajara the day after our interview—and constantly engage them in the latest and greatest USAA IT is doing. He wants them to feel they're no different than his San Antonio–based team.

That's a huge bonus, in his view. With these strategic relationships, USAA IT can scale up productivity in a snap—because Schwartz readily admits that USAA can't recruit for internal talent fast enough to meet the demands his organization continues to face.

His team of 2,500 IT professionals doesn't feel threatened that their jobs could move offshore. In the rare event that IT transitions more work to its vendors and the San Antonio team needs to shift to handle new responsibilities, IT retrains them and moves them into their next role.

As evidence that Schwartz is not looking to reduce his U.S. presence, the company announced in September 2013 that it would expand its IT operation in Plano, Texas, investing more than $31 million and bringing 600 or so new IT workers to the Dallas–Fort Worth area by 2018.

Through all these changes, Schwartz has kept an eye toward diversity as well. But there's still work to be done, Schwartz said. He wants to grow and encourage more women in IT. He wants more veterans in his workforce. He wants a more agile and diverse IT workforce.

And he's big on millennials. "I hate going to conferences where they speak badly about millennials," Schwartz said. "I think they're awesome. They might work differently, and they might think differently. We think that's an advantage, and we embrace that here."

The people issues were the fourth wall to building a more solid IT structure. And that structure functions as well as it does because of that structure's foundation: culture.

■ ■ ■

Think back to the boot-camp simulation, Zero-Day PT, that Schwartz encourages his staff—especially the newer employees—to participate in. He ties it to *mission*, a term that's often overused in the corporate world but has a direct, personal resonance with the employees at USAA and the people USAA serves. For practical purposes, think of *mission* as synonymous with *vision*.

When USAA CEO Joe Robles opens town hall meetings with employees, he starts with the company's mission statement. Then comes a video testimonial from one of its members—like Zero-Day PT, another tangible connection to the work they do and the lives and experiences of their members.

When Schwartz runs IT briefings, he talks about everything through the lens of military families. How can USAA improve its products and services to help members? What can USAA do to further increase availability? It all comes back to customer service.

And it's not "rocket science," as he said. Put your customers first, and you'll win in the marketplace. That's hard to do as a publicly traded company, but as an interinsurance exchange, USAA can actually live and breathe it, without the quarterly pressures of Wall Street.

USAA isn't the only company in that position, but it's more of an exception than a rule. Schwartz constantly reinforces the advantages of that and the company's mission-oriented focus—even if it's not innate to everyone right away. "I haven't worked at other companies, but I've hired a lot of people who have. Until they've worked here, they don't get why we're so passionate, either," he said. "Quite frankly, it's hard to put your finger on it. This is a different, special kind of company."

A core part of that mission is the collaboration between top executives. Schwartz is emphatic about his organization's role as an enabler of the business. "IT doesn't own the strategy—that falls to our business partners," Schwartz said. "But if you're an enabler, you can influence and guide and show what's possible and be effective change agents."

But that type of structure and mutual respect doesn't happen by itself. Schwartz credits his success to a few key efforts. The first is his team's ethic of focusing on their business partners' needs and how technology can enable them. The second is their own effort to master their understanding of USAA's processes. Finally, Schwartz and his team demonstrate their performance when talking with internal customers. "They know we're trying to reduce time to market, always trying to get better. We show our metrics—the good and bad. We can show year-over-year improvement," he said. "That really helps build that relationship. They know we're here to solve those business challenges."

And that's instructive for IT leaders looking to build the right relationships with the C-suite. "If CIOs follow that approach, they don't have to talk about getting a seat at the table," Schwartz said. "They'll just have it."

ABOUT THE CIOS

Chapter 1: Filippo Passerini

Filippo Passerini is group president, Global Business Services (GBS) and CIO at Procter & Gamble (P&G). He and his team of 6,000 colleagues are responsible for delivering more than 170 services and solutions to the company's employees in 75 countries worldwide.

Passerini led the integration of P&G's IT and services groups to form GBS, one of the largest and most progressive shared services organizations in the world. The GBS focus is on *transforming the way business is done*—improving productivity and efficiency to drive value, growth, and competitive advantage for P&G. Innovative in structure, scope, and philosophy, GBS has saved the company more than $1 billion to date.

Passerini has more than three decades of business-building experience with P&G in both developed and developing markets. He has lived and worked in the United Kingdom, Latin America, Greece, Italy, Turkey, and the United States. Passerini's leadership experience includes category, country, and marketing general management, and he credits his diverse exposure to the business as one of the keys to success in partnering with cross-functional leaders.

Passerini is globally recognized as an information technology and shared services thought leader. He has received numerous awards, including the inaugural Fisher-Hopper Prize for Lifetime Achievement in CIO Leadership, Shared Service Thought Leader of the Year, and *InformationWeek*'s Chief of the Year. He is a member of the CIO Hall of Fame.

Passerini serves on the board of directors for United Rentals and is a visiting professor for the Politecnico di Milano School of Management. A native of Italy, he earned his doctorate in Statistics & Operations Research from the University of Rome. Passerini and his wife, Lucia, reside in Cincinnati; they have three children and one incorrigible cat.

Chapter 2: Rebecca Rhoads

Rebecca Rhoads leads the Global Business Services group and is vice president and CIO for Raytheon Company (NYSE: RTN). Raytheon Company, with 2012 sales of $24 billion and 68,000 employees worldwide, is a technology and innovation leader specializing in defense, security, and civil markets throughout the world. Raytheon's global headquarters is in Waltham, Massachusetts.

Rhoads was appointed to lead Raytheon's Global Business Services (GBS) group in January 2013. GBS deploys a service centralization model that drives performance and operational excellence through strategic, enterprise-wide services and solutions. She is responsible for leading the application of common resources, methodologies, tools, and support systems across the company in the areas of finance, procurement, human resources, and information technology services.

Rhoads has served as CIO since April 2001. In this role, she provides expert counsel to senior management and is responsible for information technology (IT) strategy, functions, processes, and people companywide and globally. This includes IT architecture, systems, networks, investments, information protection and assurance, and IT supplier relationships. Information technology is used in the sale, design, build, procurement, delivery, and support of all Raytheon products and services.

Previously, Rhoads was vice president of IT for Raytheon's Electronics Systems business. In this role, she was responsible for all aspects of information technology in support of business requirements, including development, direction, and implementation of segmentwide information systems. Prior to that position, she directed engineering organizations in test systems design, systems reliability, safety and product effectiveness engineering, and manufacturing engineering.

Rhoads has more than 34 years of experience within the defense industry. She began her career with General Dynamics in 1979 as an electrical engineer, designing automated test systems for RAM and Stinger missile programs. She worked in Engineering and Operations, holding various assignments of increasing responsibility at General Dynamics, Hughes, and Raytheon. In addition, Rhoads taught electrical engineering classes at California Polytechnic University in Pomona, California.

Rhoads currently serves on the Aerospace Industries Association e-Business Executive Steering Group, the CIO Editorial Advisory Board, the IBM Advisory Council for CIO Center for Leadership, and the Massachusetts Technology Leadership Council and is a Massachusetts Institute of Technology Center for Information Systems Research sponsor.

Rhoads was recognized as No. 6 on ExecRank's list of Top 50 Female CIOs for 2012. Throughout her career, she has also received numerous other awards and recognition, including Corporate America Top 100 Influential Leaders, CIO Hall of Fame, Women to Watch, Women of Distinction, Top 50 Women in Technology, and California Polytechnic University Engineering Distinguished Alumni. She was also named Boston's most powerful woman in technology on Boston.com in February 2012.

Rhoads has bachelor's and master's degrees in electrical engineering from California Polytechnic University. She also holds a master's degree in the executive management program from the University of California at Los Angeles Anderson Graduate School of Business Management.

Chapter 3: Steve Bandrowczak

Steve Bandrowczak is senior vice president for Global Business Services for Hewlett-Packard.

He oversees the charter to radically drive business transformation for Global Business Services (GBS). The GBS approach is characterized by the "playing to win" strategy, focusing on the larger strategic goals built around the clear, essential elements that determine business success—where to play and how to win. In addition, Bandrowczak is the practice leader for Business Process Operations (BPO), where he will leverage the people, infrastructure, and technology of GBS to win new business for the BPO team.

Prior to GBS, Bandrowczak was vice president and CIO of Enterprise Services IT. In this role, Steve led the organization to become a strategic partner to the Enterprise Services Group in leveraging technology to position the business for growth.

He has more than 30 years of experience as an IT professional. He has held senior IT leadership positions for various multibillion-dollar global companies, including Avaya, Nortel, Lenovo, DHL, and a privately owned SAP consulting company. He is a highly accomplished, results-driven leader with demonstrated success. Bandrowczak is a distinguished technology change leader with a proven history of delivering the highest quality of leadership in a diverse range of technologies and a track record of consistently and innovatively growing businesses and enhancing competitive positions while increasing profits.

In 2004, Steve was named one of the Top 100 CIOs by *Computerworld*. He holds a Bachelor of Science in Computer Science from Long Island University, New York. He resides with his family in Palo Alto, California.

Chapter 4: Carol Zierhoffer

Carol Zierhoffer is the principal vice president and global CIO for Bechtel Corporation, having assumed this role in September 2013. She has a broad array and depth of experience in all areas of information technology and business management, including strategy formulation, governance, program management, application development, relationship management, transformation, and innovation. Zierhoffer leads Bechtel's Global Information Systems & Technology (IS&T) organization responsible for all aspects of information technology, including deployment of technology solutions into Bechtel business lines and projects around the world. Bechtel is a global leader in engineering, procurement, construction, and project management with signature projects like the Hoover Dam, Bay Area Rapid Transit, and Hong Kong International Airport, to name a few. The Bechtel portfolio encompasses energy, transportation, communications, mining, oil and gas, and government services with projects in dozens of locations worldwide, from Alaska to Australia. Bechtel is a privately held corporation with revenue of $38 billion in 2012 and 53,000 employees around the world.

Prior to joining Bechtel, Zierhoffer was vice president and global CIO for Xerox Corporation from January 2012 to September 2013, where she was responsible for all aspects of information technology (IT), leading an organization of approximately 1,250 direct and 3,000 leveraged IT staff worldwide. She was responsible for defining strategy and executing a long-term IT plan that supports the company's transformation and growth as a provider of differentiated technology products and business services.

Prior to Xerox, Zierhoffer was vice president and global CIO for ITT Corporation from October 2008 to December 2011. She was responsible for the planning, alignment, governance, and delivery of all IT products and services for ITT. She oversaw the board of directors–approved transformation initiative to implement SAP worldwide, driving to common and efficient global processes and enterprise-wide shared services. Based on the decision to split the company into three separate publicly traded companies, she oversaw the IT and Shared Services separation to spin off Xylem, Inc. (NYSE: XYL; approximate revenue: $3.2 billion) and Exelis, Inc. (NYSE: XLS; approximate revenue: $5.9 billion). Her team completed the double spin in nine months, with the remaining ITT Corporation a $1.9 billion entity.

Zierhoffer joined ITT following a 20-year career with Northrop Grumman. She was vice president and CIO for three different Northrop Grumman sectors: Electronic Systems, Information Technology, and Mission Systems. Prior to her role at Northrop Grumman, she held management positions in IT and finance at Fidelity Investments and AVCO Systems Textron.

Zierhoffer holds a bachelor's degree in business administration from the Whittemore School of Business and Economics at the University of New Hampshire and a master's degree in Computer Information Systems from Bentley University in Waltham, Massachusetts. She is also a member of the board of directors of MedAssets, Inc., where she chairs the Information Technology Committee.

Chapter 5: Lynden Tennison

Lynden Tennison was named senior vice president and CIO of Union Pacific Corporation in February 2005. In his position, Tennison is responsible for organizing and managing the development, implementation, and operation of Union Pacific Railroad's information and telecommunications technologies.

Before his promotion, Tennison was vice president of information technologies and chief technology officer for Union Pacific Railroad.

Tennison was named to that position in 2001 and had responsibility for the application systems and architectures for the entire company. From 1998 through 2001, Tennison was president and chief executive officer of Nexterna, a technology subsidiary of Union Pacific. Nexterna develops applications and hardware solutions for the mobile asset marketplace.

Prior to joining Union Pacific in 1992, Tennison spent five years with American Airlines' SABRE division and was responsible for the Knowledge Systems organization. From 1979 through 1987, he worked on various management and technical capacities for AT&T and Southwestern Bell Telephone.

Tennison has a bachelor's degree from the University of Texas at Arlington. He is a member of the board of directors for several corporations and is involved in both church and community activities.

Chapter 6: Wayne Shurts

Wayne Shurts joined Sysco in October 2012, after serving as executive vice president and CIO for Supervalu. Prior to that, he was with Cadbury Schweppes, first serving as senior vice president, information technology, and then becoming CIO in 2008. He began his career in 1981 as a management trainee at Nabisco, where he stayed for 20 years, progressing through a series of roles with increasing responsibility, including vice president, sales operations; vice president, North American supply chain process; and vice president, e-business. He left Nabisco to become president of the Principles Group, a consulting firm, where he assisted companies such as IBM, Avaya, and Johnson & Johnson with technology-enabled business transformation strategies.

Chapter 7: Don Imholz

Don Imholz has over 30 years of experience in information technology (IT), the majority at the executive level. He has also worked outside IT with executive positions in finance, manufacturing, and supplier management, among others.

Imholz joined Centene as CIO in September 2008. His current responsibilities include managing all aspects of information technology and other shared service functions such as claims processing. His focus is on implementing several major strategic information system projects, extending the use of the Internet, and creating industry-leading business analytics to support Centene's rapid growth. The organization has won a number of awards during his tenure. Imholz is a board member of the Centene Casenet subsidiary, which develops and supports advanced medical management systems.

Prior to Centene, Imholz managed his own consulting company, working for clients across a variety of industries. One of his clients was Centene. Before that, he had a long career in aerospace, first for McDonnell Douglas and then Boeing, working in a variety of functions and positions. Executive-level assignments during his career included managing the McDonnell Douglas Information Services business unit and being CIO for all of Boeing Integrated Defense Systems. At the time of his Boeing retirement in 2008, he was responsible for all information system development and support worldwide.

Imholz holds a master's degree in information systems management and an executive master's degree in business administration, both from Washington University in St. Louis. He holds a bachelor's degree in Business Administration from the University of Missouri in St. Louis and has been honored with the UMSL College of Business Administration Distinguished Alumni Award. He has also attended executive training at the Wharton School at the University of Pennsylvania and at the Kellogg School at Northwestern University.

Imholz has been active in advancing educational initiatives. He has served on the board and is past chairman of the board of directors for the Center for the Application of Information Technology and is a member of the Advisory Board for the Master's of Information Management Program for Washington University. He serves on the Leadership Council for the UMSL Business School and has served on its Information Systems Committee. He taught extensively as part of the adjunct faculty at Webster University and developed its information systems curriculum. Imholz has also been keynote speaker for many conferences and organizations.

Imholz is also on the board of directors for the Family Resource Center, a nonprofit organization providing a broad range of social services in the St. Louis area, and on the Saint Louis Zoo Board. He is married with four grown daughters and five grandchildren and enjoys travel, golf, and reading.

Chapter 8: Sheleen Quish

Sheleen Quish retired as senior vice president of Human Resources and Information Technology at Ameristar Casinos Inc. in August 2010, following its acquisition by Pinnacle Entertainment. She became CIO for Ameristar in January 2007. In 2011, she took on additional responsibilities for HR.

Prior to joining Ameristar, Quish provided advisory services to IT and business executives through her firm, Box 9 Consulting. She previously served as vice president and global CIO for U.S. Can Company, CIO at Illinois Blue Cross, and CIO of Southeastern Mutual Insurance Company (Blue Cross Blue Shield of Kentucky), where she also oversaw various functional divisions.

Quish shares her experiences and energy with IT managers and their staffs through writing, speaking engagements, consulting, coaching, and mentoring. A graduate of the College of New Rochelle (New York), she has also been a senior consultant with the Cutter Consortium, Boston, and is an emeritus member of *CIO* magazine editorial advisory board. She also serves on the executive advisory board of *Gaming & Leisure*, the industry publication for IT professionals.

Chapter 9: Greg Schwartz

Greg Schwartz is CIO and senior vice president of information technology services for USAA, a leading financial services company headquartered in San Antonio, Texas, with offices throughout the United States and Europe. The association has been serving military families since 1922 and has become well known for its exceptional service, offering its more than 10 million members a full range of insurance, banking and investment products, financial advice and planning, and other services designed to help them meet their financial needs.

Schwartz is responsible for ensuring that USAA's information technology solutions effectively support USAA's highly mobile members and their families, and he oversees the IT systems behind the multiple channels used to serve their financial needs.

Joining USAA as a computer programmer trainee straight out of college in 1983, Schwartz has held many diverse leadership positions during his 30-year tenure, culminating with his appointment to CIO in May 2004.

In each of the years Schwartz has served as CIO, USAA has been recognized as one of the top companies to work for in *Computerworld* magazine's annual 100 Best Places to Work in IT program. In 2012, USAA ranked No. 1 on the list for the third consecutive year.

In 2010, Schwartz was named by Insurance & Technology (www .insurancetech.com) as an Elite 8 outstanding insurance technology executive. In 2013, he became the first executive to receive the honor in two industries when Bank Systems & Technology (www.banktech. com), a sibling brand to Insurance & Technology, recognized him as one of its Elite 8 banking technology executives. In 2011, *Computerworld* also named him a Premier 100 IT leader.

Schwartz has been and continues to be an integral part of his organization's efforts to advance the cause of USAA members, the association, and employees by leading major efforts such as institutionalizing project management and IT strategic planning; establishing USAA's e-commerce and customer-relationship management programs—systems that now provide product-line integration and the application infrastructure that integrate the company's diversified businesses; launching USAA.com and USAA mobile applications and their associated infrastructure; and creating a state-of-the-art innovation lab for all employees across the enterprise. He provided leadership to USAA's development and launch of Deposit@Home in 2006 and Deposit@ Mobile in 2009, two innovations that revolutionized the banking industry by enabling customers to deposit checks via PC scanners and smartphones.

Schwartz earned his bachelor's degree in management information systems from Texas State University in 1982. He earned his master's degree in finance from St. Mary's University, where he graduated with honors in 1989.

ABOUT THE AUTHORS

Dan Roberts is a 30-year veteran of the IT industry and the CEO and President of Ouellette & Associates Consulting, Inc. He is a contributing author of several books, including *Unleashing the Power of IT* (Wiley, 2013) and *Leading IT Transformation*. Dan is a frequent keynote speaker at CIO and IT industry events and is often quoted in leading industry journals. He graduated from the University of New Hampshire's Whittemore School of Business & Economics.

Since 1984, Dan's firm Ouellette & Associates Consulting, Inc., has been focused on developing the human side of technology. Believing that there has never been a better time to be in the IT profession, he is passionate about closing the IT skills gap and developing the next generation of IT leaders.

Dan is on the board of Darkhorse Benefits, the 501(c)(3) nonprofit that is helping military veteran's successfully transition into IT careers while expanding the talent pool for the IT industry.

Dan is also on the Leadership Development Advisory Board of the CIO Executive Council.

Dan has two grown children. He and his wife reside in New Hampshire and Kennebunk, Maine.

You can contact Dan at:

E-mail: droberts@ouellette-online.com

Twitter: @roberts_dan

Phone: 603-623-7373

■ ■ ■

Brian P. Watson is the former editor in chief of *CIO Insight*, where he reshaped the magazine and website to offer more actionable insights from top IT leaders. Previously he served in other editorial management roles with *CIO Insight* and *Baseline*, in addition to writing for various newspapers and magazines in the United States and Europe. More recently, he has contributed to several media outlets focused on IT leadership, including the *Wall Street Journal*'s *CIO Journal* and CruxialCIO.com.

Since 2010, Brian has served as director of business outreach for Workforce Opportunity Services (WOS), a 501(c)(3) nonprofit company that trains and develops military veterans and high-potential aspiring corporate professionals for private-sector careers. In that role, he has led business development, marketing, and communications activities for the company.

Brian earned his bachelor's degree from Bucknell University and his master's degree from Northwestern University's Medill School of Journalism, where he was awarded the highest graduate honor for integrity, leadership, and character. He and his wife live in New York City.

You can contact Brian at:

E-mail: bwatson28@gmail.com

Twitter: @brianpwatson

Phone: 312-622-0803

INDEX

167